DOES IT MATTER

Also by Alan Watts

Behold the Spirit
Beyond Theology
The Book
Cloud-hidden, Whereabouts Unknown
The Joyous Cosmology
Myth and Ritual in Christianity
Nature, Man and Woman
Psychotherapy East and West
The Spirit of Zen
The Supreme Identity
Tao
This Is It
The Way of Zen
The Wisdom of Insecurity

Also by Alan Watts from New World Library

Eastern Wisdom, Modern Life
In My Own Way
Still the Mind
What Is Tao?
What Is Zen?

DOES IT
MATTER

Essays on Man's Relation to Materiality

Alan Watts

New World Library
Novato, California

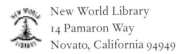

New World Library
14 Pamaron Way
Novato, California 94949

Text design and typography by Tona Pearce Myers

Library of Congress Cataloging-in-Publication Data
Watts, Alan, 1915–1973.
Does it matter? : essays on man's relation to materiality / Alan Watts.
   p.   cm.
Originally published: New York : Pantheon Books, 1970.
ISBN 978-1-57731-585-8 (pbk. : alk. paper)
1. Conduct of life. I. Title.
BJ1581.2.W36 2007
170—dc22   2007028537

First New World Library printing, November 2007
ISBN-10: 1-57731-585-5
ISBN-13: 978-1-57731-585-8
Printed in the United States on acid-free, partially recycled paper

New World Library is a proud member of the Green Press Initiative.

10 9 8 7 6 5 4 3 2 1

To Robert B. Shapiro

CONTENTS

FOREWORD

This book consists of a series of recent essays on man's relationship to the material world—to what we call nature, the physical environment, the body, and substantial matter. In using such words, I am at once aware that all of them are philosophical and abstract concepts. Equally so are notions that "reality" is in fact mental or spiritual. For I am trying to talk about something which is not talk, and which words and other symbols only represent. Alfred Korzybski called it the nonverbal or (with a delightful *double-entendre*) "unspeakable" world.

Reality is, of course, neither matter nor spirit. It is a percept, not a concept, and everyone knows what it is in the sense that one knows how to breathe without the least knowledge of physiology. As Saint Augustine of Hippo put it when asked about the nature of time: "I know what it is, but when you ask me I don't." Let's say (since in writing a book one has to say *something*) that reality or existence is a multidimensional and interwoven system of varying spectra of vibrations, and that man's five senses are attuned only to very small bands of these spectra. That sounds very profound and may mean nothing at all, but in reading it one should attend to the sound of the words rather than their meaning. Then you will get my point.

The point is that I am trying to focus attention on what is happening as distinct from the various ways in which it is described by means of words, numbers, and other symbols. The disease of civilization, whether Occidental or Oriental, is that we have too much of a good thing: we confuse the marvelous facility of description with what is actually going on, the world as labeled and classified with the world as it is. If I talk all the time I am not open to what anyone else has to say. Likewise, if I think (or talk to myself) all the time, I have nothing to think about except thoughts. I have less and less awareness of the world, the system of vibrations, which words and thoughts represent.

I am not an anti-intellectual. After all, I make my living by various feats of verbalization. But there is no grist for the intellectual mill if we get into a situation where thought is all about thinking, and where books are about nothing except other books.

It is for this reason that an enormous amount of current intellectual, philosophical, and even scientific discourse strikes me increasingly as absurd. It is an attempt to translate a nonlinear and multidimensional system of vibrations into a linear (alphabetical or mathematical) system of symbols; and it just can't be done. It is like trying to transport the Atlantic Ocean into the Pacific with a beer mug: however rapidly automated and cyberneticized the process may be, it is futile.

Not so long ago a professor of Harvard University said —in connection with the scandal about Timothy Leary and consciousness-changing drugs—that no knowledge is intellectually and academically respectable which cannot be put into words. Alas for the departments of music, art, dancing, and physical education! The problem is that literate and civilized people do not understand that their brains are much smarter than their minds, considering "mind" as the total system of verbal, mathematical, and notational rules by which we communicate and preserve information. Neurologists are the first to admit that their science does not by any means comprehend the nervous system, which is only to say that the brain is far more complexly organized than our coded, linear information about it. A trained organist, for example, can simultaneously keep in mind four different rhythms or melodies—one for each hand and one for each foot—but even very intelligent people can hardly cope with five, six, or seven variables at the same time. But the nervous system, in organizing all the functions of the body, is dealing with thousands of variables at once, for the brain operates intelligently without having to stop to think.

Thus every genius, who cannot *explain* how he paints, dances, or pitches a ball, is using his brain rather than his mind. Consider, for instance, the differences between Hindu and classical Western music. We start by learning to read a system of notation which limits us to a twelve-tone scale and to the rhythmic pulses of semibreve, minim, crotchet, quaver, semiquaver, and demisemiquaver, each of which, by being dotted, may be prolonged by a half of its value. The tradition of our music, because passed down through notation, is essentially *literate*, and all of it—even the most sentimental songs of love—sounds to Orientals like a military march. The Hindus use notation simply as an *aide-mémoire* for certain themes. One learns music by following the performance of a teacher, imitating the subtle interplay of his nerves and muscle with string, reed, or drum—as a result of which there are moments of ecstasy in Hindu music in which even God calls out for help.

Thus the point I am making in all these essays is that civilized people, whether Western or Eastern, need to be liberated and dehypnotized from their systems of symbolism and, thereby, become more intensely aware of the living vibrations of the real world. For lack of such awareness our consciousnesses and consciences have become calloused to the daily atrocities of burning children with napalm, of saturation bombing of fertile earth with all its plants, wild animals, and insects (not to mention people), and of manufacturing nuclear and chemical weapons concerning which the real problem is not so much how to prevent their use as how to get them off the face of the earth.

We need to become vividly aware of our ecology, of our interdependence and virtual identity with all other forms of life which the divisive and emboxing methods of our current way of thought prevent us from experiencing. The so-called physical world and the so-called human body are a single process, differentiated only as the heart from the lungs or the head from the feet. In stodgy academic circles I refer to this kind of understanding as "ecological awareness." Elsewhere it would be called "cosmic consciousness" or "mystical experience." However, our intellectual and scientific "establishment" is, in general, still spellbound by the myth that human intelligence and feeling are a fluke of chance in an entirely mechanical and stupid universe—as if figs would grow on thistles or grapes on thorns. But wouldn't it be more reasonable to see the entire scheme of things as continuous with our own consciousness and the marvelous neural organization which, shall we say, sponsors it?

Metaphysical as such considerations may be, it seems to me that their issues are earthy and practical. For our radically misnamed "materialistic" civilization must above all cultivate the love of material, of earth, air, and water, of mountains and forests, of excellent food and imaginative housing and clothing, and of cherishing our artfully erotic contacts between human bodies. Certainly, all these so-called "things" are as impermanent as ripples in water, but what life, what love, what energy is there in a perfectly pure abstraction or a totally solid and eternally indestructible rock?

But I must add this afterthought. The very word "rock" comes to life in "rock-a-bye baby" and "rock-and-roll." To cleave is to split and to hold together. To start is to begin a carefully prepared course of action and to jump with surprise. "Evil" read backwards is "live." *Demon est deus inversus.*

> Heaven above, heaven below;
> Stars above, stars below.
> All that is over, under shall show.
> Happy who the riddle reads.

The essays which follow were written quite independently, and I trust, therefore, that the reader will forgive some repetition of ideas, though I have tried to be sure that they are always expressed differently. "Wealth versus Money" and "Murder in the Kitchen," with some new material added, were written for *Playboy*—that remarkable journal which, posing as a high-class girlie magazine, publishes some of the most exciting philosophical thinking in America, and thus at least exposes some six million readers to the intellectual life. "The Spirit of Violence and the Matter of Peace" was written for *Alternatives to Violence*, a symposium edited by Dr. Larry Ng, neurologist, and published by Time-Life Books. "Psychedelics and Religious Experience" was written at the request of the *California Law Review* for an issue (January 1968) devoted to the legal problems of the use and abuse of drugs. It was also delivered as a lecture to the Illinois State Medical Society.

All but one of the "Seven Short Essays" were first published in *The Bulletin of the Society for Comparative Philosophy*. "The Basic Myth" and "The Great Mandala" subsequently appeared in the late lamented *San Francisco Oracle*, the most remarkable effort as yet put forth by the Underground Press; and "D. T. Suzuki: The 'Mind-less' Scholar" appeared also in the memorial symposium published in his honor by the Eastern Buddhist Society of Kyoto. "Art with a Capital A" was written as the foreword to a catalogue for an exhibition of electronic art organized by Oliver Andrews, Professor of Sculpture at the University of California, Los Angeles. Permission to publish these essays in the present volume, from the various journals involved, is gratefully acknowledged.

Alan Watts
Sausalito, California
May 1969

WEALTH VERSUS MONEY

In the year of Our Lord Jesus Christ 2000, the United States of America will no longer exist. This is not an inspired prophecy based on supernatural authority but a reasonably certain guess. "The United States of America" can mean two quite different things. The first is a certain physical territory, largely on the North American continent, including all such geographical and biological features as lakes, mountains and rivers, skies and clouds, plants, animals, and people. The second is a sovereign political state, existing in competition with many other sovereign states jostling one another around the surface of this planet. The first sense is concrete and material; the second, abstract and conceptual.

If the United States continues for very much longer to exist in this second sense, it will cease to exist in the first. For the land and its life can now so easily be destroyed—by the sudden and catastrophic methods of nuclear or biological warfare, or by any combination of such creeping and insidious means as overpopulation, pollution of the atmosphere, contamination of the water and erosion of our natural resources by maniacal misapplications of technology. For good measure, add the possibilities of civil and racial war, self-strangulation of the great cities and breakdown of all major transportation and communication networks. And that will be the end of the United States of America, in both senses.

There is, perhaps, the slight possibility that we may continue our political and abstract existence in heaven, there to enjoy being "better dead than Red" and, with the full authority of the Lord God, to be able to say to our enemies squirming in hell, "We told you so!" On the grounds of such hopes and values, someone may well push the Big Red Button, to demonstrate that belief in spiritual immortality can be inconsistent with physical survival. Luckily for us, our Marxist enemies do not believe in any such hereafter.

When I make predictions from a realistic and hard-boiled point of view, I tend to the gloomy view of things. The candidates of my choice have never yet won in any election in which I have voted. I am thus inclined to feel that practical politics must assume that most people are either contentious and malevolent or stupid, that their decisions will usually be shortsighted and self-destructive and that, in all probability, the human race will fail as a biological experiment and take the easy downhill road to death, like the Gadarene swine. If I were betting on it— and had somewhere to place my bet—that's where I would put my money.

But there is nowhere to lay a bet on the fate of mankind. Likewise, there is no way of standing outside the situation and looking at it as an impartial, coldly calculating, objective observer. I'm involved in the situation and therefore concerned; and because I am concerned, I'll be damned if I'll let things come out as they would if I were just betting on them.

There is, however, another possibility for the year AD 2000. This will require putting our minds on physical facts and being relatively unconcerned with the United States of America as an abstract political entity. By overlooking the nation, we can turn full attention to the territory, to the actual earth, with its waters and forests, flowers and crops, animals and human beings—and so create, with less cost and suffering than we are bearing in 1968, a viable and thoroughly enjoyable biological experiment.

The chances may be slim. Not long ago Congress voted, with much patriotic rhetoric, for the imposition of severe penalties upon anyone presuming to burn the flag of the United States. Yet the very Congressmen who passed this law are responsible, by acts of commission or omission, for burning, polluting, and plundering the territory that the flag is supposed to represent. Therein, they exemplified the peculiar and perhaps fatal fallacy of civilization: the confusion of symbol with reality.

Civilization, comprising all the achievements of art and science, technology and industry, is the result of man's invention and manipulation of symbols—of words, letters, numbers, formulas and concepts, and of such social institutions as universally accepted clocks and rulers, scales and timetables, schedules and laws. By these means, we measure, predict, and control the behavior of the human and natural worlds—and with such startling apparent success that the trick goes to our heads. All too easily, we confuse the world as we symbolize it with the world as it is. As semanticist Alfred Korzybski used to say, it is an urgent necessity to distinguish between the map and the territory and, he might have added, between the flag and the country.

Let me illustrate this point and, at the same time, explain the major obstacle to sane technological progress, by dwelling on the fundamental confusion between money and wealth. Remember the Great Depression of the Thirties? One day there was a flourishing consumer economy, with everyone on the up-and-up; and the next, unemployment, poverty, and bread lines. What happened? The physical resources of the country—the brain, brawn, and raw materials—were in no way depleted, but there was a sudden absence of money, a so-called financial slump. Complex reasons for this kind of disaster can be elaborated at length by experts on banking and high finance who cannot see the forest for the trees. But it was just as if someone had come to work on building a house and, on the morning of the Depression, the boss had said, "Sorry, baby, but we can't build today. No inches." "Whaddya mean, no inches? We got wood. We got metal. We even got tape measures." "Yeah, but you don't understand business. We been using too many inches and there's just no more to go around."

A few years later, people were saying that Germany couldn't possibly equip a vast army and wage a war, because it didn't have enough gold.

What wasn't understood then, and still isn't really understood today, is that the reality of money is of the same type as the reality of centimeters, grams, hours, or lines of longitude. Money is a way of measuring wealth but is not wealth in itself. A chest of gold coins or a fat wallet of bills is of no use whatsoever to a wrecked sailor alone on a raft. He needs *real* wealth, in the form of a fishing rod, a compass, an outboard motor with gas, and a female companion.

But this ingrained and archaic confusion of money with wealth is now the main reason we are not going ahead full tilt with the development of our technological genius for the production of more than adequate food, clothing, housing, and utilities for every person on earth. It can be done, for electronics, computers, automation techniques, and other mechanical methods of mass production have, potentially, lifted us into an age of abundance in which the political and economic ideologies of the past, whether left, middle, or right, are simply obsolete. There is no question anymore of the old socialist or communist schemes of robbing the rich to pay the poor, or of financing a proper distribution of wealth by the ritualistic and tiresome mumbo jumbo of taxation. If, *if* we get our heads straight about money, I predict that by AD 2000, or sooner, no one will pay taxes, no one will carry cash, utilities will be free, and everyone will carry a general credit card. This card will be valid up to each individual's share in a guaranteed basic income or national dividend, issued free, beyond which he may still earn anything more that he desires by an art or craft, profession or trade that has not been displaced by automation. (For detailed information on the mechanics of such an economy, the reader should refer to Robert Theobald's *Challenge of Abundance* and *Free Men and Free Markets*, and also to a series of essays that he has edited, *The Guaranteed Income*. Theobald is an avant-garde economist on the faculty of Columbia University.)

Naturally, such outrageous proposals will raise the old cries, "But where's the *money* going to come from?" or "Who pays the bills?" But the point is that money doesn't and never did *come* from anywhere, as if it were something like lumber or iron or hydroelectric power. Again: money is a measure of wealth, and we *invent* money as we invent the Fahrenheit scale of temperature or the avoirdupois measure of weight. When you discover and mine a load of iron ore, you don't have to borrow or ask someone for "a thousand tons" before you can do anything with it.

By contrast with money, true wealth is the sum of energy, technical intelligence, and raw materials. Gold itself is wealth only when used for such practical purposes as filling teeth. As soon as it is used for money, kept locked in vaults or fortresses, it becomes useless for anything else and thus goes out of circulation as a form of raw material; i.e., real wealth. If money must be gold or silver or nickel, the expansion and distribution of vast wealth in the form of wheat, poultry, cotton, vegetables, butter, wine, fish, or coffee must wait upon the discovery of new gold mines before it can proceed. This obviously ludicrous predicament has, heretofore, been circumvented by increasing the national debt—a roundabout piece of semantic obscurantism—by which a nation issues itself credit or purchasing power based, not on holdings in precious metals, but on real wealth in the form of products and materials and mechanical energy. Because national debts far exceed anyone's reserves of gold or silver, it is generally supposed that a country with a large national debt is spending beyond its income and is well on the road to poverty and ruin—no matter how enormous its supplies of energy and material resources. This is the basic confusion between symbol and reality, here involving the bad magic of the word "debt," which is understood as in the phrase "going into debt." But national debt should properly be called national *credit*. By issuing national (or general) credit, a given population gives itself purchasing power, a method of distribution for its actual goods and services, which are far more valuable than any amount of precious metal.

Mind you, I write of these things as a simple philosopher and not as a financial or economic expert bristling with facts and figures. But the role of the philosopher is to look at such matters from the standpoint of the child in Hans Andersen's tale of *The Emperor's New Clothes*. The philosopher tries to get down to the most basic, simple principles. He sees people wasting material wealth, or just letting it rot, or hoarding it uselessly for lack of purely abstract counters called dollars or pounds or francs.

From this very basic or, if you will, childish point of view, I see that we have created a marvelous technology for the supply of goods and services with a minimum of human drudgery. Isn't it obvious that the whole purpose of machines is to get rid of work? When you get rid of the work required for producing basic necessities, you have leisure—time for fun or for new and creative explorations and adventures. But with the characteristic blindness of those who cannot distinguish symbol from reality, we allow our machinery to put people out of work—not in the sense of being at leisure but in the sense of having no money and of having shamefacedly to accept the miserable charity of public welfare. Thus—as the rationalization or automation of industry extends—we increasingly abolish human slavery; but in penalizing the displaced slaves, in depriving them of purchasing power, the manufacturers in turn deprive themselves of outlets and markets for their products. The machines produce more and more, humans produce less and less, but the products pile up undistributed and unconsumed, because too few can earn enough money and because even the hungriest, greediest, and most ruthless capitalist cannot consume ten pounds of butter per day.

Any child should understand that money is a convenience for eliminating barter, so that you don't have to go to market with baskets of eggs or firkins of beer to swap them for meat and vegetables. But if all you had to barter with was your physical or mental energy in work that is now done by machines, the problem would then be: What will you do for a living and how will the manufacturer find customers for his tons of butter and sausages?

The sole rational solution would be for the community as a whole to issue itself credit—money—for the work done by the machines. This would enable their products to be fairly distributed and their owners and managers to be fairly paid, so that they could invest in bigger and better machines. And all the while, the increasing wealth would be coming from the energy of the machines and not from ritualistic manipulations with gold.

In some ways, we are doing this already, but by the self-destructive expedient of issuing ourselves credit (now called debt) for engines of war. What the nations of the world have spent on war since 1914 could, with our technology, have supplied every person on earth with a comfortable independent income. But because we confuse wealth with money, we confuse issuing ourselves credit with going into debt. No one goes into debt except in emergency; and therefore, prosperity depends on maintaining the perpetual emergency of war. We are reduced, then, to the suicidal expedient of inventing wars when, instead, we could simply have invented money—provided that the amount invented was always proportionate to the real wealth being produced. We should replace the gold standard by the wealth standard.

The difficulty is that, with our present superstitions about money, the issue of a guaranteed basic income of, say, $10,000 per annum per person would result in wild inflation. Prices would go sky-high to "catch" the vast amounts of new money in circulation and, in short order, everyone would be a pauper on $10,000 a year. The hapless, dollar-hypnotized sellers do not realize that whenever they raise prices, the money so gained has less and less purchasing power, which is the reason that as material wealth grows and grows, the value of the monetary unit (dollar or pound) goes down and down—so that you have to run faster and faster to stay where you are, instead of letting the machines run for you. If we shift from the gold standard to the wealth standard, prices must stay more or less where they are at the time of the shift and—miraculously—everyone will discover that he has enough or more than enough to wear, eat, drink, and otherwise survive with affluence and merriment.

It is not going to be at all easy to explain this to the world at large, because mankind has existed for perhaps one million years with relative material scarcity, and it is now roughly a mere one hundred years since the beginning of the industrial revolution. As it was once very difficult to persuade people that the earth is round and that it is in orbit around the sun, or to make it clear that the universe exists in a curved space-time continuum, it may be just as hard to get it through to "common sense" that the virtues of making and saving money are obsolete. It may have to be put across by the most skillfully prepared and simply presented TV programs, given by scientific-looking gentlemen in spectacles and white coats, and through millions of specially designed comic books.

It will always be possible, of course, for anyone so inclined to earn more than the guaranteed basic income; but as it becomes clearer and clearer that money is not wealth, people will realize that there are limits to the real wealth that any individual can consume. We may have to adopt some form of German economist Silvio Gessell's suggestion that money not in circulation be made progressively perishable, declining in value from the date of issue. But the temptation to hoard either money or wealth will dwindle as it becomes obvious that technology will keep the supplies coming and that you cannot drive four cars at once, live simultaneously in six homes, take three

tours at the same time, or devour twelve roasts of beef at one
meal.

All this will involve a curious reversal of the Protestant
ethic, which, at least in the United States, is one of the big ob-
stacles to a future of wealth and leisure for all. The Devil, it is
said, finds work for idle hands to do, and human energy cannot
be trusted unless most of it is absorbed in hard, productive
work—so that, on coming home, we are too tired to get into
mischief. It is feared that affluence plus leisure will, as in times
past, lead to routs and orgies and all the perversities that flow
therefrom, and then on to satiation, debilitation, and decay—
as in Hogarth's depiction of *A Rake's Progress*.

Indeed, there are reasonable grounds for such fears, and it
may well be that our New England consciences, our chronic
self-disapproval, will have to be maintained by an altogether
new kind of sermonizing designed to inculcate a fully up-to-
date sense of guilt. Preachers of the late twentieth century will
have to insist that enjoyment of total luxury is a sacred and
solemn duty. Penitents will be required to confess such sins as
failing to give adequate satisfaction to one's third concubine or
lack of attention to some fine detail in serving a banquet to
friends—such as forgetting to put enough marijuana in the
turkey stuffing. Sure, I am talking with about one half of my
tongue in my cheek, but I am trying to make the deadly serious
point that, as of today, an economic utopia is not wishful thinking but, in some substantial degree, the necessary alternative
to self-destruction.

The moral challenge and the grim problem we face is that
the life of affluence and pleasure requires exact discipline and
high imagination. Somewhat as metals deteriorate from "fa-
tigue," every constant stimulation of consciousness, however

pleasant, tends to become boring and thus to be ignored. When physical comfort is permanent, it ceases to be noticed. If you have worried for years about lack of money and then become rich, the new sense of ease and security is short-lived, for you soon begin to worry as much as ever—about cancer or heart disease. Nature abhors a vacuum. For this reason, the life of pleasure cannot be maintained without a certain asceticism, as in the time and effort required for a woman to keep her hair and face in fine condition, for the weaving of exquisite textiles or for the preparation of superior food. Thus, the French distinguish between a gourmand and a gourmet, the former being a mere glutton, a trencherman who throws anything and everything down the hatch; and the latter, a fussy, subtle, and sophisticated devotee of the culinary arts.

Affluent people in the United States have seldom shown much imagination in cultivating the arts of pleasure. The business-suited executive looks more like a minister or an undertaker than a man of wealth and is, furthermore, wearing one of the most uncomfortable forms of clothing ever invented for the male, as compared, say, with the kimono or the kaftan. Did you ever try the food in a private restaurant for top brass in the offices of a big corporation? Strictly institutional. Even the most expensive nightclubs and country clubs pass off indifferent fare; and at $100-a-plate charity dinners, one gets the ubiquitous synthetic chicken, machine-raised in misery and tasting of just that.

If the behavior of increasing numbers of young people is any real portent of what may happen by AD 2000, much of this will change. Quite aside from their cavalierish styles of long hair, men are beginning to wear jewelry and vivid colors, imitating the styles of medieval and Oriental affluence that began to disappear when power shifted from the landed gentry to miserly merchants of the cities—the burghers, or bourgeoisie. Beneath such outward appearances, there is a clear change of values: rich experiences are more to be desired than property and bank accounts, and plans for the future are of use only to those who can live fully in the present.

This may sound feckless and undisciplined, as if young people (especially hippies) had become incapable of postponing gratification. Thus, it might seem that the worldwide rebellions of students are a sign that the adolescent is no longer willing to work through the period of training that it takes to become an adult. "Elders and betters" do not understand that today's students do not want to become their *kind* of adult, which is what the available training is intended to produce.

Artists have always been important prophets of social change, and the increasingly favored "psychedelic" style is anything but undisciplined. Using intense color and highly articulate detail of line and form, the exponents of this style are restoring a sheer glory to Western art that has not been seen since the days of French and Celtic illuminated manuscripts, the stained glass of Chartres, and the luminous enamelwork of Limoges. It calls to mind the jeweled gardens of Persian miniatures, the rhythmic intricacy of Moorish arabesques, and the golden filigree of Hindu textiles. Among the hippies, I know makes of musical instruments—lutes and guitars—that, for delicate ivory inlays and excellence of grain and texture, are as lovely as any works of the Italian Renaissance. Furthermore, musicians are beginning to realize that the Beatles (to take an obvious example) display a serious musical genius that puts them in line with the great Western masters, from Bach to Stravinsky, and that some of the songs of Dylan and Donovan are quite as interesting as the best lieder.

At best, then, a leisure economy will provide opportunity

to develop the frustrated craftsman, painter, sculptor, poet, composer, yachtsman, explorer, or potter that is in us all—if only we could earn a living that way. Certainly, there will be a plethora of bad and indifferent productions from so many un-leashed amateurs, but the general long-term effect should be a tremendous enrichment of the quality and variety of fine art, music, food, furniture, clothing, gardens, and even homes—created largely on a do-it-yourself basis. Mechanical mass pro-duction will provide utilities, raw materials, tools, and certain foodstuffs, yet will at the same time release us from the neces-sity for much of the mass-produced trash that we must now buy for lack of time to make anything better—clothes, dishes, and other articles of everyday use that were made so much more exquisitely by "primitives" that they now adorn our museums.

Historically, luxuries of this kind could be afforded only by shameless aristocrats exploiting slave labor. Though still exploiters, the bourgeoisie were timid newcomers, often had Protestant guilty consciences and, therefore, hid their wealth in banks and did their very best to pretend that successful busi-ness is an ascetic and self-sacrificing way of life. But by AD 2000, there need be no slaves but machines, and it will then be our urgent duty to live in that kind of luxurious splendor that depends upon leisurely devotion to every form of art, craft, and science. (Certainly, we have long forgotten that a *schola*, or school, is a place of leisure, where those who do not have to grub for a living can apply themselves to the disinterested pur-suit of knowledge and art.) Under such circumstances, what exuberant styles of life will be cultivated, for example, by af-fluent Negroes under no further pressure to imitate the white bourgeoisie?

The style of life will be colorful and elegant, but it will not, I feel, exhibit the sheer gluttony and greed of certain notorious aristocracies of the past. Speaking perhaps only half seriously, by AD 2000, most of Asia will have followed the lead of Japan and be laced with superhighways and cluttered with hot-dog stands, neon signs, factories, high-rise apartment buildings, huge airports, and swarms of Toyotas, with every fellah and coolie running around in a Western business suit. On the other hand, America, having had all this and being fed up with it, will abound with lamaseries and ashrams (but coeducational), expert players of the sitar and koto, masters of Japanese tea ceremony, schools for Chinese calligraphy and Zen-style gardening—while people stroll around in saris, dhotis, sarongs, kimonos, and other forms of comfortable and colorful clothing. Just as now the French are buying sourdough bread flown by jet from San Francisco, spiritually starved Tibetans and Japanese will be studying Buddhism in Chicago.

That this is not quite a joke might be inferred from the amazing increase of interest among American college students in Oriental mysticism and other "non-Western" studies, as courses in Afro-Asian cultures are now often classified. Obviously, this interest is not unconnected with the widespread use of psychedelic drugs. This is not, as is often suggested, a substitute for alcohol: it is much more an adventure, an exploration of new dimensions of experience, all the more attractive for being esoteric and in defiance of authority. To repeat, students tend to be much more interested in experiences than in possessions, feeling that their parents' way of experiencing both themselves and the world is in some way sick, impoverished, and even delusive. Certainly—and precisely because their parents have for generations confused symbol with reality, money with wealth, and personality (or ego) with the actual human organism.

And here's the nub of the problem. We cannot proceed with a fully productive technology if it must inevitably Los Angelize the whole earth, poison the elements, destroy all wildlife, and sicken the bloodstream with the promiscuous use of antibiotics and insecticides. Yet this will be the certain result of the technological enterprise conducted in the hostile spirit of a conquest of nature with the main object of making money. Despite the growing public alarm over the problems of soil erosion, pollution of the air and water, and the deterioration of crops and livestock raised by certain methods of industrial farming, little is as yet being done to develop an ecological technology—that is, a technology in which man has as much respect for his environment as for himself.

In this regard, many corporations—and even more so their shareholders—are unbelievably blind to their own material interests; for the ill effects of irresponsible technology are appearing so rapidly that we can no longer simply pass the buck to our children. Recent investigations, both here and in England, show that the actual operators of chicken factories avoid eating their own produce; it may be as well for the appetites for their absentee shareholders that they do not know too much about raising hens in batteries. Does anyone care what happened to the taste of fruits and vegetables, or mind particularly if apples and tomatoes are often sprayed with wax to improve their looks? (I just scraped an apple, very gently, to prove it.) Is it either good business or good living to buy an $80,000 home in Beverly Hills and inhabit a miasma of exhaust fumes? (In Paris, last May, we didn't mind the tear gas much; just used to L.A.) Is it even sane to own a Ferrari and, twice daily, jangle one's nerves and risk one's life by commuting from Norwalk, Connecticut, to Madison Avenue, New York? And what about

the view from the plane between San Francisco and Seattle—
acres and acres of brown Oregon hills dotted with nothing but
tree stumps?

It is an oversimplification to say that this is the result of
business valuing profit rather than product, for no one should
be expected to do business without the incentive of profit. The
actual trouble is that profit is identified entirely with money, as
distinct from the real profit of living with dignity and elegance
in beautiful surroundings. But investors take no long-term responsibility for the use of their capital: they clip coupons and
watch market statistics with regard only for monetary results.
They see little or nothing of the physical operations they have
financed, and sometimes do not even know that their own funds
are invested in the pithy potatoes they get for dinner. Their
actual experience of business is restricted to an abstract, arith-
metical translation of material fact—a translation that automatically ignores textures, tastes, sights, sounds, and smells.

To try to correct this irresponsibility by passing laws (e.g.,
against absentee ownership) would be wide of the point, for
most of the law has as little relation to life as money to wealth.
On the contrary, problems of this kind are aggravated rather
than solved by the paperwork of politics and law. What is necessary is at once simpler and more difficult: only that financiers,
bankers, and stockholders must turn themselves into real people and ask themselves exactly what they want out of life—in
the realization that this strictly practical and hard-nosed question might lead to far more delightful styles of living than those
they now pursue. Quite simply and literally, they must come
to their senses—for their own personal profit and pleasure.

The difficulty is that most of our very high-ranking business executives live in a closed world. They are wafted from

their expensive but unimaginative homes and clubs to offices of dreary luxury, wherein they are protected and encapsulated by secretarial staffs. They read only what is filtered through by underlings and consort only with others who are in the same Bigelow-lined traps. It is almost impossible for people outside their caste to communicate with them directly; for they are victims of a system (also a ritual) so habitual, so complex, and so geared in to the whole corporate operation that the idea of changing it seems as preposterous as rewiring the human brain. Actually, this life is a form of role playing with the reward of status; its material rewards are meager—for one reason, because it is tiring and time consuming. But to suggest that one should change an established role is to be understood by the player as suggesting that he become someone else, and this affront to his imaginary ego is such that he will cling passionately to a role of high status, however much it may be frustrating his natural and material inclinations. This would, perhaps, be commendable, if the role being played fulfilled important responsibilities to society; and many businessmen do, indeed, feel themselves to be doing just that. But their closed world prevents the realization that in the vast, long-range world of material events, they are highly irresponsible—both to their children and to themselves. This is precisely why so many of their own children drift off to the dubious adventures of Haight-Ashbury or the East Village: they find the high life of Scarsdale or Atherton, Lake Forest or Beverly Hills inconceivably dull.

Hopefully, there are signs that some of these very children are getting through to their parents, since it's tough to put a secretary between yourself and your son. Is there any historical precedent for the revolt of a younger generation against the older on the present scale? So widespread? So radical—in politics, morals, religion, dress, art, and music? So vociferous—with such powerful techniques of communication as are now available? I do not believe that the elders will ultimately reject the children; it's against nature. But to make peace, the elders will have to move a long, long way from their present position.

Less hopeful are the prospects of a change of attitude in the ranks of successful blue-collar workers, who, as now organized in the once very necessary but now highly reactionary labor unions, constitute the real and dangerous potential for American fascism. For the unions operate under the same confusion of symbol and reality as the investors: the wage is more important than the work and, because all must conform to union hours and (mediocre) union standards, any real enthusiasm for a craft is effectively discouraged. But a work force so robotized is all the more inviting its replacement by machinery, since a contrivance that won't work must inevitably be replaced by one that will. The basic assumption of unionism was not the dignity but the drudgery of labor, and the strategy was, therefore, to do as little as possible for as much pay as possible. Thus, as automation eliminates drudgery, it eliminates the necessity for the unions, a truth that is already extending up to such "high-class" unions as the musicians'. The piper who hates to play is replaced by a tape, which does not object when the payer calls the tune. If, then, the unions are to have any further usefulness, they must use their political pressure, not for a greater share of profits (based on rising prices to pay for rising wages) but for total revision of the concept and function of money.

The fear that adequate production and affluence will take away all restraint on the growth of population is simply against the facts, for overpopulation is a symptom of poverty, not wealth. Japan, thus far the one fully industrialized nation of Asia, is also the one Asian country with an effective program of population control. The birth rate is also falling in Sweden, West Germany, Switzerland, and the United States. On the other hand, the poorer nations of Asia and Africa resent and resist the advice that their populations be pruned, in the feeling that this is just another of the white man's tricks for cutting down their political power. Thus, the one absolutely urgent and humane method of population control is to do everything possible to increase the world's food supply, and to divert to this end the wealth and energy now being squandered on military technology.

For, from the most realistic, hardheaded, self-interested, and tactically expert point of view, the United States has put its Armed Forces in the control of utterly incompetent strategists—a bunch of essential "bad shots" who do not know the difference between military skill and mere firepower, who shoot at mosquitoes with machine guns, who liberate countries by destroying their territories, whose principal weapon is no weapon at all but an instrument of mutual suicide, and whose political motivations, based on the puerile division of the world into "good guys" and "bad guys," cannot allow that enemies are also people, as distinct from demonic henchmen of a satanic ideology. If we were fighting in Vietnam with the honest and materialistic intention of capturing the wealth and the women of the land, we would be very careful to leave it intact. But in fighting for abstract principles, as distinct from material gain, we become the ruthless and implacable instruments of the delusion that things can be all white, without the contrast of black.

Timothy Leary was not so wide of the mark when he said that we must go out of our minds (abstract values) to come to our senses (concrete values). For coming to our senses must, above all, be the experience of our own existence as living organisms rather than "personalities," like characters in a play or a novel acting out some artificial plot in which the persons are simply masks for a conflict of abstract ideas or principles. Man as an organism is to the world outside like a whirlpool is to a river: man and world are a single natural process, but we are behaving as if we were invaders and plunderers in a foreign territory. For when the individual is defined and felt as the separate personality or ego, he remains unaware that his actual body is a dancing pattern of energy that simply does not happen by itself. It happens only in concert with myriads of other patterns—called animals, plants, insects, bacteria, minerals, liquids, and gases. The definition of a person and the normal feeling of "I" do not effectively include these relationships. You say, "I came into this world." You didn't; you came *out* of it, as a branch from a tree.

So long as we do not effectively feel this to be so, there is no motivation for forms of politics that recognize the interdependence of all peoples, nor for forms of technology that realize man's inseparability from the entire network of natural patterns. How, then, is the sense of self to be changed? By scientific education? It convinces the intellect but not the emotions. By religion? The record is not hopeful. By psychotherapy? Much too slow. If anything is to be *done* about it, and done in time, I must agree with Aldous Huxley (and with the sober and scholarly Arthur Koestler in his *Ghost in the Machine*) that our only resort may be psychopharmacology—a chemical, a pill, that brings the mind to its senses.

Although I have experimented very sympathetically with such methods (LSD, etc.), I would be as reluctant to try to change the world with psychedelics as to dose everyone indiscriminately with antibiotics. We do not yet know what ecological damage the latter may have done, how profoundly they may have upset certain balances of nature. I have, therefore, another and perhaps equally unacceptable suggestion.

This is simply that nothing be *done* about it. Shortly before his death, Robert Oppenheimer is said to have remarked that the whole world is, quite obviously, going to hell—adding, however, that the one slim chance of its *not* going to hell is that we do absolutely nothing to stop it. For the greatest illusion of the abstract ego is that it can do anything to bring about radical improvement either in itself or in the world. This is as impossible, physically, as trying to lift yourself off the floor by your own bootstraps. Furthermore, the ego is (like money) a concept, a symbol, even a delusion—not a biological process or physical reality.

Practically, this means that we stop *crusading*—that is, acting for such abstract causes as the good, righteousness, peace, universal love, freedom, and social justice, and stop fighting against such equally abstract bogeys as communism, fascism, racism, and the imaginary powers of darkness and evil. For most of the hell now being raised in the world is well intentioned. We justify our wars and revolutions as unfortunate means for good ends, as a general recently explained that he had destroyed a village in Vietnam for its own safety. This is also why we can reach no genuine agreement—only the most transitory and unsatisfactory compromises—at the conference tables, for each side believes itself to be acting for the best motives and for the ultimate benefit of the world. To be human, one must recognize and accept a certain element of irreducible rascality both in oneself and in one's enemies. It is, therefore, an enormous relief to realize that these abstract ambitions are total nonsense and to see that we have been wasting untold psychic and physical energy in a fatuous enterprise. For when it is understood that trying to have good without evil is as absurd as trying to have white without black, all that energy is released for things that *can* be done. It can be diverted from abstract causes to specific, material undertakings—to farming and cooking, mining and engineering, making clothes and buildings, traveling and learning, art, music, dancing, and making love. Surely, these are excellent things to do for their own sake and not, please *not*, for one's own or anyone else's improvement.

MURDER IN THE KITCHEN

A living body is not a fixed *thing* but a flowing *event*, like a flame or a whirlpool: the shape alone is stable, for the substance is a stream of energy going in at one end and out at the other. We are particular and temporarily identifiable wiggles in a stream that enters us in the form of light, heat, air, water, milk, bread, fruit, beer, beef Stroganoff, caviar, and *pâté de foie gras*. It goes out as gas and excrement—and also as semen, babies, talk, politics, commerce, war, poetry, and music. And philosophy.

A philosopher, which is what I am supposed to be, is a sort of intellectual yokel who gapes and stares at what sensible people take for granted, a person who cannot get rid of the feeling that the barest facts of everyday life are unbelievably odd. As Aristotle put it, the beginning of philosophy is wonder. I am simply amazed to find myself living on a ball of rock that swings around an immense spherical fire. I am more amazed that I *am* a maze—a complex wiggliness, an arabesque of tubes, filaments, cells, fibers, and films that are various kinds of palpitation in this stream of liquid energy. But what really gets me is that almost all the substance of this maze, aside from water, was once *other* living bodies—the bodies of animals and plants—and that I had to obtain it by murder. We are creatures rearranged, for biological existence continues only through the mutual slaughter and ingestion of its various species. I exist solely through membership in this perfectly weird arrangement of beings that flourish by chewing each other up.

Obviously, being chewed up is painful, and I myself do not want to be chewed up. Thus the whole scheme bothers my conscience. If the morticians don't get me first, will my being eaten up by germs and worms be fair compensation for the countless cows, sheep, birds, and fish that I have consumed during my lifetime? I wonder: is this entire biological arrangement of mutual mayhem an insane and diabolical contraption that moves faster and faster to a dead end? I have seen plants infested with greenfly, one day swarming with plump and succulent little bodies, the next—grey dust on dry stalks. Life seems to be a system that eats itself to death, and in which victory equals defeat.

Man can easily go the way of the greenfly, for as he becomes expert in technology, he is seen to be more predatory than locusts or piranha fish. He is devouring, destroying, and fouling the whole surface of the planet: minerals, forests, birds, insects, fresh water—all are being converted into suburbs and sewage, rust and smog. Meanwhile, the total conquest of his natural enemies from tigers to bacteria allows his own race to swarm itself out of space; and, through fear of his own rapacious kind, he wastes a huge proportion of his wealth in the manufacture of weapons, ever more deadly and ever more obsolete as technical skill increases. Many prehistoric animals became extinct because of overdeveloped weaponry—the saber-toothed tiger through the unmanageability of its immense shearing teeth, and the titanothere through the unsupportable weight of its colossal nose-horn.

One can, perhaps, accept the idea that as the individual dies, so must the species. Thereafter, the energy of the universe will appear in new patterns and guises, and dance to different rhythms. The show will always go on, but must the going on be so intense an agony? Must the price of life always be soft, sensitive flesh and nerve squirming under the crunch of sharp teeth? If so, then, as Camus said, the only serious philosophical problem is whether or not to commit suicide.

Again, therefore, the philosopher wonders: Short of suicide, is there any way out of this vicious circle of mutual killing, which, in any case, seems to be suicide in the long run? Is there any way of avoiding, mitigating, or generally cooling this system of murder and agony which is required for the existence of even the most saintly human being?

Vegetarianism, for example, is no solution. Years ago the Indian botanist Sir Jagadis Bose measured the pain reactions of plants to cutting and pulling. To say that plants don't really *know* that they are in pain is only to say that they can't put it into words. When I pointed this out to a strictly vegetarian Buddhist, the famous Reginald H. Blyth, who wrote *Zen in English Literature*, he said, "Yes, I know that. But when we kill vegetables they don't scream so loud." In other words, he was just being easy on his *own* feelings. Buddhist and Hindu monks have carried the attitude of *ahimsa*, or harmlessness, to the extreme of keeping their eyes on the ground when walking—not to avoid the temptations of lovely women, but to avoid trampling on beetles, snails, or worms that might lie in the path. Yet this is at root an evasion, a ritual gesture of reverence for life which in no way alters the fact that we live by killing.

Searching my own conscience as to how I should respond to this predicament, I find three answers.

The first is to admit that deciding to live is deciding to kill, and make no bones about it. For if I have really made up my mind to kill I can do it expertly. Consider the agony of being halfway decapitated by a reluctant executioner. Death must be as swift as possible, and the hand that holds the rifle or wields the knife must be sure. (Incidentally, you wouldn't want your surgeon to be so sorry and concerned for you that his hand trembled when he opened your abdomen.)

The second is that every form of life killed for food must be husbanded and cherished on the principle of "I love you so much I could eat you," from which it should follow that "I eat you so much that I love you." This principle has been most seriously neglected by hunters in the past, and by industrial farmers and fisherman today. To cite only two examples, modern techniques of whaling are in danger of abolishing whales, and industrial poultry-farming is flooding the market with nonchickens and pseudo-eggs. The wretched birds are raised in wire cell-blocks, fed on chemicals, are never allowed to scratch around in the sun, and taste just like that. Whatever is unlovable on the plate was unloved in the kitchen and on the farm.

The third is expressed by Lin Yutang as follows: "If a chicken has been killed, and it is not cooked properly, that chicken has died in vain." The very least I can do for a creature that has died for me is to honor it, not with an empty ritual, but by cooking it to perfection and relishing it to the full. Any animal that becomes me should enjoy itself as me.

The proper love of animals and plants, and of other materials upon which our life depends, is nurtured in the kitchen. Yet one look at the average American or British kitchen shows that it is not a place of love. Stuck off in a constricted corner of the house, it looks like a bathroom or surgery—white, cold, and dowdy, though sometimes glossy and militantly clean. Such kitchens are, like toilets, mere conveniences, where food is dutifully rendered chewable and assimilable because it is good for you. And everything that comes from such kitchens tastes as if it were good for you—scrubbed with soap, wiped off with rubbing alcohol, and thoroughly disinfected in boiling water. This is a rule of almost mathematical exactitude: colorless kitchen = tasteless food.

These abominable kitchens are not the result of poverty. They reflect the fact that the richest and most powerful civilization on earth is so preoccupied with saving time and making money that it has neither taste for life nor capacity for pleasure. The commonly accepted notion that Americans are materialists is pure bunk. A materialist is one who loves material, a person devoted to the enjoyment of the physical and immediate present. By this definition, most Americans are abstractionists. They *hate* material, and convert it as swiftly as possible into mountains of junk and clouds of poisonous gas. As a people, our ideal is to have a future, and so long as this is so we shall never have a present. But only those who have a present, and who can relate to it materially and immediately, have any use for making plans for the future, for when their plans mature they will enjoy the results. Others, with their eyes fixed on the tomorrow that never comes, will bolt down all times present—forever—along with a vitamin-enriched styrofoam called "bread."

Much may be learned about a civilization from its staple food, which, in our case, is supposed to be bread. Real bread is a solid and crusty substance with an aroma evoking visions of farm kitchens, flour mills, sacks of wheat, and rolling, waving fields of grain, gold and gentle in the lazy heat of a late summer afternoon. Few Americans have such associations and our bread does not suggest them, being a virtually weightless compound of squishy and porous pith injected with preservatives and allegedly nutritive chemicals. It is not so much white as ideally and perfectly colorless, and approximates—as nearly as human genius can manage it—to the taste of absolute nothingness. It is a compact of air bubbles, each contained in a film of edible plastic which has been synthesized from wheat or rye as one gets casein from milk. In contact with liquid, be it gravy or saliva, this plastic film disintegrates at once into a cloying and textureless paste exactly like the revolting white slime which is fed to babies, and which most babies, quite understandably, spit back into the spoon.

To begin with, the wheat is grown, unloved, by industrial farming over millions of featureless and treeless acres in such wastelands as Kansas and Nebraska, and is sprayed by airplane with Flit and Bugdeath. It is then shaved off the face of the earth with immense mechanical clippers, winnowed, and ground into a flour which, by washing with detergents and stewing in disinfectants, is converted into tons of pancake makeup. In vast automated baking factories these mountains of pure chalk-dust are mixed with pantothenic acid, pyridoxine, para-aminobenzoic acid, and artificial flavorings, whereafter the whole mass is bubbleized, stabilized by heating, sliced, wrapped in wax paper, and shipped out in the form of sleazy cushions which are unfortunately too small and too perishable for use as bolsters. You may think I am exaggerating, but according to a recent issue of *Scientific American* someone has patented a process for the manufacture of continuous "bread" which flows through electronic ovens like toothpaste from a tube. "A steady stream of ingredients is mixed, the dough is kneaded, and carbon dioxide is pumped into it to make it rise. (Yeast may be added, but only for flavor.)" The resultant product has no end-crusts.

Several years ago a reader complained about this so-called bread to *Consumer Reports*, a generally admirable magazine designed to protect its subscribers from cheating in the marketplace. But instead of submitting the product to the judgment of experienced chefs and gourmets, *CR* called in dieticians and chemical analysts who reported that this miserable substance was indeed "rich in vitamins and nutritious minerals."

Here is the nub of the problem: we confuse diet with medicine and cooking with pharmacology, and thus it comes to pass that the classes of dietician and cook are mutually exclusive— the former judging by the test tube and the latter by nose and tongue. Labels on food packages read just like labels on proprietary medicines. I have just taken a package of ordinary gelatine from the shelf, and it reads:

> ANALYSIS: Protein 85–87%. Moisture 12–14%. Ash 1.0-1.2%. Fat 0. Sodium 90 mg./100 Gm. or 1 mg. per serving. Carbohydrate 0. Calories per envelope 28.

You may not have the slightest idea what this means, but with all that small, scientific-looking print and decimal points it sure must be good for you. Our judgment of food is theoretical and mathematical rather than material, which is my reason for saying that Americans are not materialists but abstractionists.

The mutually exclusive roles of dietician and cook are nowhere more apparent than in such institutions as hospitals and colleges. In my particular work it is frequently my fate to have to take lunch or dinner in the student-union cafeterias of universities all over the country. All are identical. Icebox lettuce with a glob of cottage cheese and a wedge of canned pineapple. Slices of overdone and warmed-over beef that have suffered for hours in some electronic purgatory, coated with a gravy made of water, library paste, and bouillon cubes. Peas, corn, and carrots—boiled. The pie is a sickening slab of beige goo, flavored with artificial maple sugar, in a crust of reconstituted cardboard, topped with sweetened shaving cream squirted from an aerosol bomb. The effect of this fare on the intellectual life of the nation must be catastrophic. Since university politics are mainly a matter of interdepartmental feuding, the home economics and dietetics people are clearly way out on top, having conspired to deprive historians and mathematicians, linguists and anthropologists, of all zest for life by habituating them to the notion that such supernaturally uninspired meals are the proper diet for scholars.

The problem is that the dieticians who actually supervise such "cooking"—as well as the hapless agents of the FDA and the Department of Agriculture who inspect the forced and faked-up products that go into it—can indeed prove that it contains the proper amount of proteins, carbohydrates, minerals, and vitamins. But this is like judging the worth of music in terms of decibels and wave frequencies. "This record certified noninjurious to the human ear." Certainly, it is all *good* for us— in the sense that it will enable us to put up with existence for a reasonably long time. Even sex is becoming acceptable for the same reason: it is good for you; it is a healthy, tension-reducing "outlet"—to use Kinsey's statistical term for counting orgasms—and some wretched hygienist will soon figure out the average person's minimum daily requirement of outlets (0.428 would be three times a week) so that we can screw with a high sense of duty and freedom from guilt. Watch your outlet count and keep a chart beside the bed.

But just exactly what is the "good" to which we aspire through doing and eating things that are supposed to be good for us? This question is strictly taboo, for if it were seriously investigated the whole economy and social order would fall apart and have to be reorganized. It would be like the donkey finding out that the carrot dangled before him, to make him run, is hitched by a stick to his own collar. For the good to which we aspire exists only and always in the future. Because we cannot relate to the sensuous and material present we are most happy when good things are expected to happen, not when they are happening. We get such a kick out of looking forward to pleasures and rushing ahead to meet them that we can't slow down enough to enjoy them when they come. We are therefore a civilization which suffers from chronic disappointment—a formidable swarm of spoiled children smashing their toys.

To our ears, therefore, the assertion that time does not exist must sound insane. Time, we say, is money, and, boy, that's for real! Yet it is impossible to be in the right state of mind for cooking, or eating or for any other art or pleasure without realizing that time is purely abstract. There is indeed such a thing as "timing"—the art of mastering rhythm—but timing and hurrying are as mutually exclusive as cooks and dieticians. Clock time is merely a method of measurement held in common by all civilized societies, and has the same kind of reality (or unreality) as the imaginary lines of latitude and longitude. The equator is useless for stringing a rolled roast. To judge by the clock, the present moment is nothing but a hairline which, ideally, should have no width at all—except that it would then be invisible. If you are bewitched by the clock you will therefore have no present. "Now" will be no more than the geometrical point at which the future becomes the past. But if you sense and feel the world materially, you will discover that there never is, or was, or will be anything except the present.

For the perfect accomplishment of any art, you must get this feeling of the eternal present into your bones—for it is the secret of proper *timing*. No rush. No dawdle. Just the sense of flowing with the course of events in the same way that you dance to music, neither trying to outpace it nor lagging behind. Hurrying and delaying are alike ways of trying to resist the present, and in cooking they invariably show up in the form of spoiled food. To try to have time, that is, to move as quickly as possible into the future, gives you abstract food instead of real food. Instant coffee, for example, is a well-deserved punishment for being in a hurry to reach the future. So are TV dinners. So are the warmed-over nastinesses usually served on airplanes, which taste like the plastic trays and dishes on which they are served. So is that meat which is not roasted but heated through in thirty-second electronic ovens. So are mixtures of grape juice and alcohol, prepared in concrete vats, pretending to be wine.

Even our fruits and vegetables have been rushed, so that however magnificent an apple may seem to the superficial judgment of the eye, it is hard to find one that is not simply wet pith under the skin, and most potatoes taste of the same nothingness as bread. For a while I thought this might be because I had ruined my palate with too much tobacco, but when I recently returned to my father's garden in England I found both apples and potatoes as real as they had been to the untainted palate of a child.

Abstractionists would, if possible, save time by eating the menu instead of the dinner, which is almost what actually happens in those restaurants where one reads:

FILET OF COLORADO MOUNTAIN TROUT, gently sauteed in breadcrumbs to a delicate golden brown, with fresh garden peas simmered in butter, light and crisp French-fried potatoes, and lemon wedge.

Sometimes there is even a colored photograph to whet the appetite for the dismal anticlimax of the reality. The last time I ran into this, in a restaurant where they had the nerve to keep an open kitchen, the "Filet of Colorado Mountain Trout" was a severe rectangle of some off-white substance which rattled when it hit the grill.

Another way of eating the menu is preferring money to wealth—a psychic disorder directly related to the hallucination that time is a physical reality. To be fair, there are still some substantial and excellent products for sale in our supermarkets, but if you are bewitched by money, what happens? You take your loaded cart to the cashier, who clicks out a long strip of paper and says, "Thirty dollars and twenty-five cents, please!" You are suddenly depressed at having to part with so much "wealth"—not realizing that your wealth is now in the shopping bags and that you are going to walk out with it. For the money was a future, a "promise to pay," an abstraction now converted into present and substantial reality—and you are unhappy because you have exchanged the expectation of good things to come for actual goods! Just as time is a way of measuring motion, money is a measurement of material wealth and power, a system of bookkeeping, and when this is not understood, a nation with vast material abundance can—as in the Depression—starve for lack of purely symbolic cash.

In a civilization devoted to the strictly abstract and mathematical ideal of making the most money in the least time, the only sure method of success is to cheat the customer, to sell various kinds of nothingness in pretentious packages. Spray your watery tomatoes with wax to make them look real. But then, having made the money, there is nothing real to buy with it because everyone else is cheating in the same way.

One would suppose that in this richest of all nations prosperous stockbrokers and admen, plumbers and electricians, would knock off work and drive full pelt for routs, banquets, and orgies that would make the high life of ancient Rome look like potluck supper at a Methodist social. But as things are, the well-heeled blue-collar people go home to gurgle down cans of an alcoholic soft drink misnamed "beer," and watch television over hamburgers and ketchup. The white-collars live it up by getting anaesthetized on martinis and then, perhaps, going to reasonably good French or Italian restaurants with neither taste nor appetite for the fare. In New York I often stay at a small hotel on a street of celebrated European restaurants. Every morning at six I am awakened by the banging and thumping of garbage trucks which carry away tons of an immense slosh of leftovers, in which I can just make out the forms of lobster thermidor, oysters Rockefeller, *filet mignon aux champignons*, poached salmon, *moules marinière*, and *coq au vin*, slobbered over with almost all the vegetables served the previous evening—since no one ever eats them. Excellent as the cuisine may be, restaurants in America serve for the eye and not for the stomach, because abstractionists delight in the initial lift of fancy menus and vastly overloaded dishes— suited only to the appetites of growing boys, who cannot afford to eat in such places. The customer wants anticipation; he has no capacity for fulfillment.

The heart of the matter is that we are living in a culture which has been hypnotized with symbols—words, numbers, measures, quantities, and images—and that we mistake them for, and prefer them to, physical reality. We believe that the proof of the pudding is in the chemical analysis, not in the eating. This is largely the result of an educational system which is overwhelmingly literary and mathematical, which prepares everyone to be clerks and bureaucrats, and provides apprenticeship in arts of material competence only reluctantly—for those considered too stupid for intellectual advancement.

This is not sentimentalizing about the "dignity of labor." It is saying that a culture is hardly a culture at all when it does not provide for the most sophisticated training in the fundamental arts of life: farming, cooking, dining, dressing, furnishing, and love-making. Where these arts are not cultivated with devotion and skill, time to spare and money to spend are useless. The shops are empty of all but trash, thrown together by slaves working joylessly for cash with one eye on the clock. Thus there are virtually no jobs to be had for those who delight in expert workmanship in producing the necessities of everyday life. The jet aircraft and scientific instruments are marvelous, but houses, cars, fabrics, bathtubs, carpeting, jewelry, suits, chinaware, beds, and lighting fixtures are simply phenomenal failures of human imagination. (Incidentally, if you want truly elegant glassware for the kitchen—jars, funnels, decanters, bottles—buy it from a dealer in laboratory equipment.)

In the world of symbols and abstractions—understood in terms of separate and disjointed words—the human person is an isolated *thing* among other things. Oneself is therefore experienced as a lonely center of consciousness and action living inside an envelope of skin. This envelope is an abrupt boundary between oneself and an alien universe, and the main task of life is to join forces with other lonely ones for the "conquest of nature"—that is, for the violent subjugation of an enemy universe to our wills. Hence, also, our talk of "the conquest of space." But as a result of this feeling we are destroying our environment and fouling our own nest. Increasingly, the world around us *looks* as if we hated it.

Yet this particular feeling of personal existence is a delusion. The special branch of science which studies the relation of living beings to their environments—ecology—shows beyond doubt that the individual organism and its environment are a continuous stream, or field, of energy. To draw a new moral from the bees and the flowers: the two organisms are very different, for one is rooted in the ground and broadcasts perfume, while the other moves freely in the air and buzzes. But because they cannot exist without each other, it makes real sense to say that they are in fact two aspects of a single organism. Our heads are very different in appearance from our feet, but we recognize them as belonging to one individual because they are obviously connected by skin and bones. But less obvious connections are no less real.

There are, for example, no strings connecting the widely separated molecules in your own hand. There is no visible material joining the individual stars into the formation which we recognize as *a* galaxy. But civilized human beings are alarmingly ignorant of the fact that they are *continuous* with their natural surroundings. It is as necessary to have air, water, plants, insects, birds, fish, and mammals as it is to have brains, hearts, lungs, and stomachs. The former are our external organs in the same way that the latter are our internal organs. If then, we can no more live without the things outside than without those inside, the plain inference is that the words "I" and "myself" must include *both* sides. The sun, the earth, and the forests are just as much features of your own body as your brain. Erosion of the soil is as much a personal disease as leprosy, and many "growing communities" are as disastrous as cancer.

That we do not feel this to be obvious is the result of centuries of habituation to the idea that oneself is only the envelope of skin and its contents, the inside but not the outside. The extreme folly of this notion becomes clear as soon as you try to imagine an inside with no outside, or an outside with no inside.

To see this clearly is to acquire a new attitude to the physical world which includes, first, a profound respect for the intricate interconnections between all creatures, upon which each of them depends, and second, a love for and delight in that world as an extension of your own body. True, this world maintains itself by mutual killing and eating; but with this new attitude murder in the stockyards and on the farms will not be compounded with the murdering of food in the kitchen—or of the landscape by ill-conceived housing, or of the air and sunlight by industrial and automotive farting.

Thus the one absolutely essential requirement for the art of cooking is a love for its raw materials: the shape and feel of eggs, the sniff of flour, or mint, or garlic, the marvelous form and shimmer of a mackerel, the marbled red texture of a cut of beef, the pale green translucence of fresh lettuce, the concentric ellipses of a sliced onion, and the weight, warmth, and resilience of flour-dusted dough under your fingers. The spiritual attitude of the cook will be all the more enriched if there is a familiarity with barns and vineyards, fishing wharves and dairies, orchards and kitchen gardens. One of my most heart-lifting and persistent memories is of a row of oak-leaf lettuce seen at midnight under a full moon—jigsaw patterns of edible jade refreshed with minute drops of dew. I think also of hiding, as a child, between rows of scarlet runner beans upon sticks, opening the large pods that had gone to seed, and crunching the raw purple-mottled beans. After much searching, discovering a long, heavy pod concealing itself in the vines.

With this attitude it is practically impossible to chuck food carelessly into boiling water or to roast, distractedly by the clock, without eager peeks into the oven to sniff and baste. A good cook broods over the range like a doting mother, or like an alchemist distilling the elixir of immortality from rare herbs. The preparation must be as delightful for its own sake as the feast, if the feast is to be worth eating. For the cook is, after all, a priest offering sacrifice, and the stove is an altar. There must be the same devotion and absorption as in performing a magical rite, or, if you are not accustomed to such things, as in giving the utmost pleasure to a gorgeous woman, in bringing the full sound out of an exquisite musical instrument, or in watching the leisurely sail of your golf ball from the tee to the green.

One can sense the style and attitude of ritual in almost any action that is done expertly, with full attention to the present— as when a surgeon handles his instruments at an operation, when a jeweler repairs a watch, or when pilots prepare for the takeoff of a plane. Such is the fascination (i.e., magic) of ritual that Americans, who pride themselves on being folksy, plain, and direct, will go abroad in droves to witness a coronation ceremony, and be thrilled when a *mâitre d'* comes to a cart beside the table and prepares *crêpes suꝣette* with flaming brandy. We are, indeed, so starved for ritual that thousands of staunch Protestant businessmen who would be horrified at solemn high mass in the Presbyterian church will nevertheless join the Freemasons and the Shriners to wear exotic robes and take part in archaic ceremonies.

Happily, there is still in our souls a primitive and essential awe for that central god of the kitchen whose name is Fire. Americans, unlike the British and the French, have an abundance of spacious fireplaces in their homes, and, over the last twenty years, the paterfamilias has been increasingly drawn to the rites of the barbecue and its ceremonial appurtenances—the chef's hat, the apron, and the long skewers, fork, and turner. A return to this timeless form of cooking is a clear sign that all is not yet lost, and that we are never going to have any real appetite for the kind of meals—now available in some drive-ins—where your order is dialed and delivered electrically in sixty seconds. My faith in human nature tells me that our very nerves will force us to realize that there can be no taste at the table without love in the kitchen.

Now, the center of almost every civilized home in the Western world is a barren space called the living room, which is anything but lively. At one time it was more correctly known as the parlor, that is, the "talking place" where one received honored visitors, and as such it was firmly walled off, used only on special occasions, smelled vaguely musty, and contained little besides chairs and sofas, a cabinet of curios and pretty plates, and a few pictures. The family *lived* elsewhere: if one had no servants, in the kitchen; otherwise, in the library or the boudoir or the nursery. But with the virtual extinction of servants and the increasing cost of space, homes have suffered a weird transformation. Logically, we should have abandoned the pretentious luxury of the parlor and moved into roomy kitchens. Instead, we have moved into the parlor and reduced the kitchen to a bathroomlike appendage. This has enabled us to maintain the illusion that we could still afford servants, or at least a cook, preparing meals off-scene to be presented at the table as if, say, roast lamb were a "dish" created miraculously out of nothing.

It is in such ways that civilization, as we have worked it out, is a system of screens which conceal the connections between events. Just as roast lamb is a presentation at the table without visible connection with kitchen, cooking, or sheepherding, so, also, children simply arrive amongst us without visible connection with sexual intercourse or parturition. Bacon, as found packaged in the supermarket, gives no intimation of pig, and steaks appear as if they were entities like apples, having no relation to the slicing of dead cattle. To remove such screens is held to be as offensive and vulgar as to relieve one's bowels in the gutter of a public street.

Similarly, the living room is the place where a family appears, to itself and to others, "on stage" as ladies and gentlemen who do not farm, kill, cook, wash, shit, or fuck—all four-letter words! A home should indeed bear some relation to the human organism which it houses: as mouth and rectum are at opposite ends of the alimentary canal, kitchen and can should be kept well apart. (It should be noted in passing that one of the great pleasures of Japanese civilization is the communal bathtub, but that the bathroom is kept quite separate from the *benjo*, except in modern hotels, where each room has a private bath.) But when the segmentation of living goes too far, when our various organic functions are performed in separate and private boxes, we appear on stage in our homes only as people who eat (rather apologetically), drink, sit, and talk. The rest of the house is a sort of "unconscious"—and a cramped one at that—into which our more biological functions are repressed.

This arrangement accords, however, with the illusion that one's actual self is a distinct mental entity, a soul or ego, which inhabits and is supposed to control the body, but does not really belong to it. This nonbiological self is an abstraction, a complex of words, symbols, and ideas—a *persona*, or mask, instead of a living being—and this is why the parlor, the chatter box, is the principal room in the homes of a civilization positively dedicated to this illusion.

The misnamed living room is indeed, then, a withdrawing room into which we withdraw not so much from the table, after dinner, as from biological existence. Such withdrawal would be honest and conscious if the room in question were a library, a place set apart for the intellectual life. But in a nation which supports not much more than one thousand legitimate bookshops, few living rooms are libraries. By and large the central and principal room of the house is a great wasted space, cluttered with heavy, ungainly, and expensive furniture to support the inflexible and creaking frames of people who are ashamed of their bodies.

Let us begin with chairs. A chair is properly an adjunct to a table, and a table is a clean, raised surface used for serving food so that we do not stumble over the dishes nor have our meals interrupted by unmannerly dogs, cats, and infants. But standing alone in a living room the chair is an absurd perch, a type of surgical support for bodies unadapted to the ground. As for the bulbous forms of overstuffed armchairs and couches, one would suppose that they had been designed as containers for the shipment of rocs' eggs. Any rest and comfort that they afford is offset by the effort of heaving them around to vacuum the floor, by their initial expense, and by the cost of transporting their monstrous bulk when moving house. However bechintzed and camouflaged, they have about the same aesthetic value as gun emplacements.

The same strictures, incidentally, apply to most beds, with their ponderous head- and footboards, and the dense arabesques of wires and springs which support their elephantine mattresses. They require an additional waste of space in the form of (usually dreary) bedrooms with an area large enough to squeeze around these prodigious pads in the daily chore of making them. For rest and privacy the ideal solution seems to me to be a large windowed closet where the whole floor is covered with foam rubber and carpeted. On retiring, pillows and quilts, or electric blankets, are laid upon the floor, Japanese style, and returned to concealed shelves in the morning.

The problem, then, is that our homes exhibit the same lack of material competence and biological intelligence as our cooking and clothing. They are made for posturing persons instead of living organisms. And it is not as if the posturing persons were putting on a really good show; they are witlessly and cheaply reproducing the lifestyle of lords and ladies who lived in an age of abundant space and plentiful slaves, of aristocrats who, under the influence of Christian puritanism, could pretend that they never had to stoop so low as to cook or to perform those other biological activities expressed with four-letter words. And this lifestyle is as obsolete and vestigial as the buttons on the sleeves of our coats.

As a product of the ambitious *petite bourgeoisie*, I have for years been under the illusion that one should aspire to something "better in life" than the material arts which maintain and beautify our human biology. This something "better" is always cerebral, abstract, and symbolic: to be a writer, clergyman, lawyer, politician, financier, professor, or philosopher—anything that would keep my *hands* out of life. For myself, I am not bitter about it; *some* people have to be brahmins, and I think

I have done a fair job of it, though I doubt if I could survive a month in the "state of nature" without brawny and skillful peasants to help me. The intellectual, literate, and theoretical life has its place as one of several differentiated vocations or—it must be admitted—castes. Rigid and anachronistic as it became, the Hindu principle of caste was based on the essentially sound idea that the community needs intellectuals (*brahmana*), governors and soldiers (*kshatriya*), merchants and businessmen (*vaisya*), and laborers, skilled and unskilled (*sudra*). But what if almost *everyone* aspires, or is taught that he should aspire, to the more cerebral styles of life? That will put everyone in the parlor and no one in the kitchen.

My answer is "Back to the kitchen!" It should supplant, and even abolish, the living room as the center of the home. The practical difficulty is that no one wants to go back to the kinds of kitchens that we have—to piles of filthy dishes, Formica tabletops, chromium-trimmed appliances, bathtub sinks, obese black-and-white ranges, and enormous streamlined refrigerators designed to go through the air at two hundred miles per hour, all cramped into the smallest space consistent with the unfortunate necessity of having to eat. Let us grant that, in recent years, at least the appearance of kitchen appliances has changed for the better (at considerable extra cost), but most British and American kitchens are still exemplary for their "practical ugliness," not for lack of means but for lack of imagination.

The first step, as many architects have rather halfheartedly shown us, is to take out the wall between kitchen and living room. (I am not writing for the few who can begin a new home from scratch, or for those who already have spacious kitchens. They will readily see how to apply my principles to their own circumstances.) The second is to partition off a small area for a scullery, consisting of a shelf or shelves for dirty dishes and an automatic dishwasher. If possible, the same area can contain washing machine, dryer, and deep-freeze units. Beyond this, the object is to merge the kitchen and living room into a single unit, functionally and aesthetically, as a place where cooking, eating, drinking, talking, singing, or listening to music are all in place.

Halfhearted architects divide the "kitchen area" from the "living area" with a bar, which has much to be said for it if the bar is something more than a convenience for serving drinks or eating breakfast, though even this has the advantage of allowing the cook, whether wife or husband, to stay with the party or the family while preparing the meal. The important point is, however, that appetite is marvelously increased by watching and smelling the preparation of food. This is the attraction of the American barbecue, and of Japanese bars for *tempura* (deep-fried shrimps and vegetables), *yakitori* (charcoal-broiled "kebabs" on bamboo skewers), and *sushi* (small slices of chilled and perfectly fresh raw fish on patties of marinated rice, sometimes wrapped in paper-thin seaweed). This, too, is the delight of such meals cooked at the table as *sukiyaki* and *mizutake* (the former by sauteeing and the latter by simmering meat or fish with vegetables), and of such comparable Swiss preparations as cheese fondue and *fondue bourguignonne*, where chunks of sourdough bread are dipped into a communal chafing dish of hot liquid cheese, or cubes of raw beefsteak into hot oil. If, then, the kitchen is to be divided from the dining area by a bar, let the bar run immediately alongside the range, barbecue pit, and a generous slab of chopping board—all with a hooded vent overhead. Here family and guests can sip their preprandial drinks and have their appetites whetted by the scents, sights, and rituals of preparing the meal. (Note in passing that the problematic "smell of cooking" is not given off by cooks who refrain from the merciless boiling of vegetables and from the reuse of old oil. Stocks for soups and gravy should be prepared early in the day, long before guests arrive.)

The kitchen as a whole should resemble a delicatessen rather than a surgery. There should be an ample central table of plain well-scrubbed wood which may be used both for eating and preparation; and, at least in my ideal kitchen, strings of onions, sausages of hard salami, cheeses in wax or muslin, and basketed bottles of Spanish and Italian wine would hang from beams overhead. As no true lover of books keeps them hidden in cupboards, so the basic food supplies that need no refrigeration should not have their comforting presence concealed. Flour, sugar, salt, rice, and other grains should be kept in stoppered glass jars, preferably of the kind used in laboratories. Spices, canned goods, boxes, and bottles should adorn the walls on open shelves, covered only with sliding glass panels if protection from dust be necessary. Practically, this avoids the nuisances of hunting through cupboards and banging into the corners of their open doors, and allows one to locate and review supplies at a glance. Skillets and saucepans, together with such utensils as the pancake turner, cooking spoon and fork, strainers, skewers, and snail pans should dangle from well-ordered wall hooks and not be flung into drawers.

Allow no utensil in the kitchen that is not in some sense a work of art—not prettified stuff but exquisitely functional, such as the best wooden spoons from Italy, made from lemonwood, enameled casseroles from Sweden, Solingen kitchen knives, terra cotta bowls from Mexico, Revere ware or heavy copper saucepans from England, or a fine Chinese *wok* (pan for stir-frying) with its turner and spoon. Tinny and plasticky utensils from Woolworth's or the supermarket are as out of place as an electric harmonium in a cathedral. Beware, however, of a superfluity of gadgetry—especially of those appliances which take more time to clean than they save in operation, such as that electrified pea-pod opener for "the cook who has everything."

Although we move inexorably into an electronic age, I am content with this magic for refrigeration and dishwashing, and for powering a blender. Technologically, it is not yet as satisfactory for cooking as gas and charcoal. Heat cannot be reduced instantly, as with gas, and saucepans must therefore be removed from the burner and set down elsewhere. Give me a table-top gas range of stainless steel, and a windowed oven-broiler about four feet from the floor so that I don't have to grovel to baste the turkey, or prostrate myself to inspect a steak. Those electronic ovens which render a roast chewable in seconds, though perhaps allowable for vegetables, are the peculiar abominations which account for the food now served on airplanes and in hospitals. They have no place in civilized kitchens, and the warmed-overness of their products is simply a penalty for haste.

To one side of the range I would install a charcoal pit or Japanese *hibachi* (the double size measuring about 10 by 20 inches), since with proper ventilation charcoal broiling need not be a purely outdoor affair. My friend Sumire Jacobs, a Japanese lady who is undoubtedly one of the best nonprofessional cooks in California, has a permanently installed *wok* adjoining her range, and I have been persuaded that this wide, round-bottomed frying pan should be in every kitchen, for no method of preparing vegetables is to be compared with the Chinese way of stir-frying them for from one to three minutes in a small quantity of very hot sesame or soybean oil. The *wok*, which includes an inside-fitting lid or cover, rests over the flame in a metal ring upon which it can be turned to all angles, and the Chinese use it for an immense variety of dishes. It is the most versatile of all cooking pans.

Most kitchens have utterly inadequate chopping boards—miserable little planks that pull out from above a top drawer or hang on the wall. Many lumber merchants can, however, supply solid, heavy chopping board by the square foot, made of ¾ inch strips of hardwood, cut across the grain, glued together and finely sanded. At least 2½ by 3 feet of one's working area should be made of this material, and, ideally, it should replace all working surfaces except the draining area by the sink, which should be tile or stainless steel. There is something about Formica tops with chrome edges which, if only by way of an imaginative brain, nullifies the taste of anything prepared upon such alien and unnatural surfaces.

But what is it about plastics in general? It is rumored that beautiful plastic objects can be made, but the plastics which ordinarily enter the kitchen are vile in color, obnoxious in shape, and repulsive in texture. I am contemplating, for example, a receptacle for washing dishes, about 18 inches square and 9 inches deep. It is rounded at all corners and slobberingly rolled outwards along the edges as if it were just about to turn itself inside out. The material is vaguely soft, so that when filled with water and lifted it sags to one side and spills. It feels like thick, cold, greasy leather, except the grease doesn't come off on your hands. You suspect, rather, that molecule-size particles are penetrating your skin through the pores. The color is a pale dusty green that tried to be fluorescent and failed. As an artist friend once said, "There are two kinds of green: green and damn green." This is not the pale green of sunlight through spring leaves; it is *mal-de-mer* or corpse green, not unlike the color of people attempting to survive on a macrobiotic diet or to be vegetarians on the basis of standard British or American cuisine.

Objects of this kind also come in frozen-custard pink, hepatitis yellow, and baby-soap blue. Plastic bowls of this last color are now to be found in bathrooms all over Japan, replacing the small wooden tubs which used to be used for washing and sploshing oneself before getting into the deep bath for a long soak. Japan is in fact in an epidemic state of plasticitis. Visit any public beach. The high-water mark, once a wavy line of seaweed, driftwood, and shells, is now a rubbish trail of torn plastic bags, squeeze bottles, bloated sandals, and abandoned toys—miles and miles of it, all plastic, all virtually indissoluble by the normal elements. The Japanese love of nature! They even have plastic antimacassars, printed like white lace, to hang over the backs of overstuffed chairs. One can only hope that this is the swan song, the last gasp, the final *reductio ad absurdum* of the Japanese-Edwardian style of dress and furnishing which has been making official, genteel, and urban Japan look silly for fifty years.

Alchemically, plastic is related to the salve with which witches were supposed to rub their bodies before their diabolical Sabbath, whereon they were alleged to insult the divine order of nature by transforming themselves into dogs with human torsos and all manner of Brueghelesque monsters—fish-bats, spider-rats, porcupine-snakes, and pigeon-frogs. Human substance became an infinitely malleable goo, obedient to every whim of perverse imagination. Plastic is the same negative spiritualization of matter: it can mock any shape and be transformed into textureless everything. Plastic glasses can flatten the taste of beer and wine, and make even water feel as if it had

been distilled. Plastic plates will cause the juicy essences of a
steak to evaporate instantly and transform all fish into boiled
cod. For lack of weight and substance they slide about on the
table, and they cannot be preheated without wilting.

Plastic typifies the whole mock-materialism of industrial
civilization, and now that it is being used by surgeons to make
spare parts for the human body, we may anticipate the day when
people survive interminably as plastic reproductions of themselves. On the principles of wax casting or embalming with
formaldehyde, we may some time be able to inject the body
with a liquid plastic that will flow through the veins and capil-
laries, the alimentary tract and intestines, and finally along the
nerves into the brain, following the forms of every neuron and
cell. The treated individual will then be dropped into an acid
bath in which all natural flesh will be dissolved and the liquid
plastic firmed up by a fixative mixed in the acid, while the new
heart is fed with synthetic, acid-resistant blood—and in those
days Disneyland will inherit the earth.[1]

For Disneyland exists "as a mystery and a sign," the land of
the fake and the home of the bogus, prototype of the world to
come. Even the birds in the trees are plastic, and sing through
their hinged beaks with tiny loudspeakers. Plastic deer, bears,
elephants, and bunny rabbits stand along the banks of artificial
lakes and rivers, monotonously wagging their mechanical
heads. Tourists, traveling by river boat through simulated
jungle, have the thrill of seeing a plastic hippopotamus shot
with a blank cartridge, and a varnished *papier-mâché* replica of

---

[1] Stanford Research Institute has already predicted that Orange County, the home
of Disneyland, will become the vital center of the whole Los Angeles–Southern
California subtopia.

the Swiss Family Robinson's tree house which vibrates perpetually to the recorded music of an oom-pah-pah band (on a loop tape) going "Pom-pitty bom-pitty pom-pitty bom-pitty" for ever and ever. Though it takes hours to go through all the "shows," a decent restaurant—let alone a bar—is nowhere to be found, since this is strictly sodapop-culture, where one must subsist upon hamburgers, hot dogs, ice cream, popcorn, or Fred Harvey–type meals.

For the true significance of Disneyland is that it reflects our notions of children—what they are, what is good for them, and what will please them. Children are a special class of human beings which came into existence with the industrial revolution, at which time we began to invent a closed world for them, a nursery society, wherein their participation in adult life could be delayed increasingly—to keep them off the labor market. Children are, in fact, small adults who want to take part in the adult world as quickly as possible, and to learn by doing. But in the closed nursery society they are supposed to learn by pretending, for which insult to their feelings and intelligence they are propitiated with toys and hypnotized with baby talk. They are thus beguiled into the fantasy of that happy, carefree childhood with its long sunny days through which one may go on "playing"—in the peculiar sense of not working—for always and always. This neurotic suppression of growth is outwardly and visibly manifested in the child's toy world of plastic and tin, of miniaturized won't-work guns, airplanes, cars, kitchen ranges, dinner sets, medical kits, and space rockets, designed so to entrance them that they will keep out of the way of adults. Yet every suburban mother must, at 5 PM, ruin her disposition for cooking by engaging in a knock-down drag-out battle with her brood, which has, by that time of day, strewn the entire house with the wreckage of these baubles, compelling them to gather up the remains and fling them into closets and drawers bemixed with half-sucked lollipops and bubble gum.

In truth, children resent their nursery world but are given no opportunity to go beyond it. They cannot participate in their father's work because he goes away to an office or factory. Most mothers shoo their children out of the kitchen: it is too small to contain them, and she is rushed and harried by the fray of the clean-up battle or by getting home late from a bridge game or half-time job. A common solution is to get the children fed before their father gets home for dinner or guests arrive, polluting their palates with hot dogs and ice cream washed down with Coca-Cola, while they sit mesmerized in front of the TV absorbing cutie-pie cartoons or mayhem.

My father, too, went to the office, except for a brief period during the Depression when he was farming rabbits at home and allowed me to work with him. But, miserably small though it was, my mother never kept me out of the kitchen. Whenever possible she let me help a little, but otherwise I acquired a basic understanding of cooking just by being able to watch.[2] I never had to do any serious cooking until I was thirty-four, living alone for a year, and then discovered that the art was somehow in my bones. A year or two later, wintering in a New England farmhouse where the kitchen was the only warm room in the place, I really got down to it and have never been able to give up. When writing, I like to work from about 6:30 AM until 4 PM, and then switch from the abstract to the concrete by going to see what the market has to offer for dinner. Work in

---

2 She goes down to history as author, under her maiden name Emily Mary Buchan, of *Easy Dishes for Small Income* (London, Routledge, 1910).

the kitchen brings me down from intellectual clouds to re-establish contact with things of the earth, and my wife, though an excellent cook in her own right, humors me by letting me have the run of the kitchen, usually cleaning up as I go along.

Because our home is an ex-ferryboat, the kitchen is still something of a galley. Nevertheless, dinner guests have a way of drifting in with their cocktails to chatter and watch the proceedings, and, as an innate show-off, I have no objection. However, the basic reason is that an attractive kitchen is a primordial center of human gravity. Everyone wants to know "what's cooking." The kitchen is no mere utility room. It is as much a place for sculpture, paintings, and plants as anywhere else in the house, and I have abandoned the usual white or brown color schemes for royal purple, cobalt blue, and emerald green with a nine-faced mask of Vishnu—"resplendent Indweller, seed of all that is"—on the wall above the range.

Being a place of transformation, of alchemy, the kitchen should have some atmosphere of magic—perhaps a shrine for one's tutelary kitchen god, or exotic objects and utensils from far-off lands. I like a kitchen to put me in mind of the description of an alchemist's shop in the *Arabian Nights*—

> Chinese and Indian drugs, medicines in leaf and powder, salves, pomades, collyriums, unguents and precious balms; . . . choice spices and every kind of aromatic thing, musk, amber, incense, transparent tears of mastic, unrefined benzoin, and essence of every flower, camphor, coriander, cardamoms, clovers, cinnamon from Serendibis, Indian tamarind and ginger, and a quantity of bird olives, those with the thin skins and sweet flesh filled with juice and coloured like blond oil.

Everyone knows, of course, that the natives of Serendibis (Ceylon) and Kashmir, Sikkhim and Samarkand, Tahiti and Tashkent, find their own lives as matter-of-fact as ours, though for them there is magic in the names of London and Paris, New York and San Francisco—and for many of us, too. Yet if the magic of exotic things and places is only a projection of the imagination, it shows at least that one *has* imagination—or shall I say imagicination, the power to radiate magic. As a romanticist and lover of the exotic without qualms of conscience I still hanker for

> Quinquereme of Nineveh from distant Ophir
> Rowing home to haven in sunny Palestine,
> With a cargo of ivory,
> And apes, and peacocks,
> Sandalwood, cedarwood, and sweet white wine.

Thus I have promised myself that if and when I reach the age of seventy, I shall retire to a mountain slope near the ocean and raise a small garden of herbs—culinary, medicinal, and psychedelic. Beside the garden I shall build a redwood barn where bunches of drying plants will hang from the beams, and where long shelves will be lined with jars and bottles of dulcamara and spikenard, ginseng and aloeswood, lobelia, mandragora, and cannabis, pennyroyal, horehound, and meadowsweet. There also I shall maintain an alchemist's laboratory-cum-kitchen with a library, and if the world presses too much in on me, my wife will respond to unwanted visitors in the words of Chia Tao's poem "Searching for the Hermit in Vain"—

> The master's gone alone
> Herb-picking, somewhere on the mount,
> Cloud-hidden, whereabouts unknown.

CLOTHES—ON AND OFF

For most of my life I have been in rebellion against the various riggings of cloth which authority or fashion have constrained me to wear. It is largely the fault of the British, who, as arbiters of style in men's clothing, have foisted upon mankind the most ridiculous and uncomfortable forms of dress ever invented. From Beau Brummel to the tailors of Saville Row and Bond Street, the British stylists have sold their absurd uniforms of tweed and worsted to the whole world. They have stripped the Japanese of their kimonos, the Ceylonese of their sarongs, the Hindus of their dhotis, and the Levantines of their kaftans—so that today a Japanese businessman goes about looking like a bag too large for its contents, and, on formal occasions, appears in the black Edwardian cutaway or morning coat with striped pants. Since the Japanese are relatively short, especially in the legs, the coattails reach well below their knees and one expects them at any moment to hop around and caw.

I know all about it, for I was born and educated in England. When I was sent off to boarding school they trussed me in an Eton suit. This sartorial disaster consists of tight dark grey pants, a black waistcoat or vest with lapels and cloth-covered buttons, and a black monkey-jacket known as a bum-freezer, obviously designed for the purpose of making the

bottoms of small boys more readily presentable for flogging.
The pants were held up by suspenders (which we called braces)
and the socks by garters (which we called suspenders). The
shirt was usually of an off-white striped flannel to which was at-
tached, with collar-buttons or studs, an immense starched white
collar worn outside the jacket. With this went either a black top
hat or a "boater" straw hat, ribboned with the school colors.
Ours were salmon-pink with a white fleur-de-lis at the front.
The outfit had nothing to recommend it, either practically or
aesthetically. It was too hot in summer and too cold in winter.
The starched collars became both grubby and dented after even
an hour's wear. The straw hat blew away in the wind, and
sometimes had to be secured with the foppery of a hat guard—
a thin black cord dangling between the brim of the hat and the
lapel of the jacket.

On our attaining the height of 5 feet 7 inches, the uniform
was changed to black striped pants with the black Marlborough
jacket (i.e., the normal jacket of the adult male), and the Eton
collar was replaced by a starched wing collar of the type that
used to be worn with formal evening dress, plus a black silk
necktie. On the street we carried gloves with silver-topped
canes or neatly rolled umbrellas. But it was still absurd.

Let me catalogue the follies of Western man's British-
inspired dress:

Item: pants or trousers are entirely unsuited to male anatomy,
insulting by ignoring the *membrum virile*. (Into which leg do
you put it?) They are appropriate for very shapely women.

Item: jackets are clumsily shaped for folding and packing,
and invariably emerge creased and crumpled from the suitcase.
There is no conceivable use for lapels or for buttons on the
sleeves, the latter being a survival from the days when fancy

uniforms had rows of buttons on the sleeves to discourage their use for wiping the nose.

Item: the male suit violates the nature of cloth by forcing it to fit the shape of the body. Woven materials are essentially rectangular and resent being molded into cylindrical, conical, or hourglass forms. They like to be allowed to hang freely, and show their appreciation by conferring dignity and ease upon the wearer.

Item: the standard white shirt can hardly be folded except by an expert laundress, and has an insufferable tendency to creep up from beneath the belt and spill over the edge of the pants. Furthermore, no man should look ridiculous in any part of his clothing, and a man "caught with his pants down" in nothing but a shirt is a sight unpleasing to the eye. Especially when he is wearing black socks with garters.

Item: the necktie, even when colorful, is a sacred cow. It is a noose facilitating instant strangulation and a symbol of servitude. Restaurants which refuse admission to persons unornamented by this meaningless strip of cloth will simply lose the patronage of the increasing number of well-heeled men who wear more unconventional or colorful clothing.

Item: strong leather shoes, and especially those of the hard, shiny, and unflexible British type, are just extra weight to carry when walking, deny freedom of movement to the complex bone structure of the foot, and by airless enclosure promote sweat, stink, athlete's foot, and a black crud between the toes composed of fall-out from the skin mixed with lint from the socks. We used to call it toe-jam.

Item: starch on collars or cuffs is anathema. It scratches the skin and rots the fabric. Fortunately, we are no longer compelled to wear the starched shirt-front with formal dress, but one is amazed that men could ever have tolerated such crustacean apparel.

In sum, conventional male dress is trussing. It is tight, stiff, and constricting, and we are so habituated to it that many people feel vaguely guilty when, several hours after arising, they are still clad in some loose-fitting robe. The collar, the tie, the belt, the pants, the shoes, the tightly fitted jacket squeeze in on you with the information that you are indeed really and truly *there*. As if you didn't know. Some people get it by lying on beds of nails, by walking to the Basilica of Guadalupe on their knees, by enduring Swedish massage, or by the curious sexual kick known as "bondage," which involves being tied up with ropes in awkward positions and tickled with feathers. I am not contesting anyone's freedom to use all these devices to enhance their sense of reality or "existential authenticity," but I resent their authority over the rest of us—which compels me to go to fine restaurants, attend formal parties, and conduct business outside my home in grotesque garments which deprive me of ease and freedom and display little or no aesthetic imagination.

What about our clothes for women? Superficially, they seem to be looser and easier, and also more colorful—unless one insists upon smart black with a string of pearls. But let us take a close look at them from the feet up.

Item: high-heeled shoes, especially the patent-leather ones with long, sharp points, have obviously been designed by foot fetishists who cannot be sexually aroused unless their women grind them in the rectum or trample their bellies with this sinister footwear which calls to mind, what? A Cadillac upended on an enormous jack. A sitz bath with one leg from a grand piano. A stag beetle with an immense erection. Such shoes, especially when combined with tight skirts, compel women to walk "step-step-step-step" like inhibited mechanisms, clacking along the pavements and jarring their nerves. No natural or liberated person makes a noise when walking.

Item: nylon stockings are the most impractical legwear ever invented. They run at the slightest scratch; they are a flimsy and expensive form of frou-frou which have to be supported by

Item: a garter belt or elastic girdle arrangement with pulleys and block-and-tackle contraptions to hold said stockings in position. Although we have largely abandoned the feminine armor of laced corsets with whalebone ribbing, many women still feel flabby and undressed without the "snuggy" clutch of the girdle about their hips and buttocks. They should realize, however, that when they undress for their husbands or lovers their skins bear the herringbone imprints and sundry other dents and welts inlaid by these weird devices. Furthermore, women should not be ashamed of ample development in the *jaghana* (the Hindu word for this whole region of the body); it is particularly attractive beneath a thin waist.

Item: the brassiere is a surgical appliance which may be necessary for ladies with excessively pendulous bosoms, but otherwise it is without value except that of deception, as when falsies are used as compensation for unduly small breasts.

(Looking over my shoulder, my wife says that women, especially of the younger generation, no longer wear these monstrosities. This goes to show, however, that I am not fighting a losing battle and that in this, as in many other matters, the young are beginning to show unexpected good sense.)

Item: there is a common species of women's outer dress most aptly termed a frock. It is usually made of flimsy, flower-printed rayon with skirt descending a little below the knees. Upon elderly ladies with bulging stomachs (by whom this garment is chiefly worn) it is an undignified abomination supposed to be reminiscent of frilly girlishness, and often goes with a hat resembling a flattened-out hydrangea. Please, ladies, just don't do it.

Item: women's gowns are, in general, held together by tiny, irritating devices such as zippers in unreachable places, minute snappers, and hook-and-eye myopicisms where the eye is often nothing more than an infinitely small loop of invisible thread. How do single women, without husbands or maids, get themselves zip-snap-hooked together?

Final item: hats, applying to both women and men. There are two basically sensible hats, one made of fur for protection against the cold as found in Canada, Alaska, and Russia; the other for protection against rain, the large flat cone- or mushroom-shaped hats made of rice straw, worn by coolies and monks in the Far East, obviating the necessity for carrying umbrellas. Otherwise, hats are absurd and pretentious superstructures without practical value or aesthetic charm. Upon entering restaurants and other places where they must be ritually doffed (and one might discuss at great length the etiquette and symbolism of donning and doffing the hat), these useless lids must, at least by men, be parked in a cloakroom for from twenty-five to fifty cents, thus costing an urbane owner who frequently dines out for business or pleasure at least $65.00 per annum.

Consider such hats as the topper, the derby or bowler, the Homburg, or the stiff visored cap affected by the military and the police. Even when well fitted they afflict slight welts on the brow, promote baldness, and express a pompous attitude to life. Philosophers and theologians have given all too little attention to the vice of pomposity, which is, at root, the folly of taking oneself seriously. As a liberated person walks soundlessly, like a cat, he also takes himself lightly. Pomp, which comes from the Greek word *pompos*, meaning the leader of a procession, also suggests by onomatopoeia the ridiculous "oom-pah-pah" noises made by the enormous saxhorns used in military bands and thus, by further association, the booted stomping, rattling, and slapping of military drills. Effective soldiers, such as guerillas and commandos, move without the slightest sound and thus never announce their coming. The affectation of military pomp by the German armies is one reason why they lost two world wars, and why the Americans are failing in Vietnam. Pomp is probably a compensation for sexual inadequacy, but must not be confused with the easy swagger of the male who enjoys his own body. Americans win wars only to the extent that they employ the tactics of Indians. Tact is, after all, silence.

> Stoop not, dear men, to demean your souls
> By going round in black inverted bowls
> Whereunder, crawling cooped, you live and die.
> Take for your hat the wide dome of the sky;
> Far nobler headpiece than a bulbous lid
> Beneath whose firmament no stars are hid,
> Nor any winds of heaven find entrance there
> To blow the dust of dandruff from your hair.

So much, then, for hats.

Now—unless some zoologist can dig up a weird exception—humans are the only living beings who wear clothes. They are also the only beings who laugh, for humor is the property of humanity and consists, essentially, in not taking oneself seriously. (Consider the situation of someone chasing a hat blown off by the wind.) People can laugh at themselves because they know, deep down, that their lives are a big act, a put-on.

This may get us into the depths of mysticism, but every person knows, tacitly, that he is God in disguise. Not, perhaps, the universal monarch of Jewish and Christian imagery, but at least the inmost and ultimate Self of Hinduism, the Actor who plays all the roles, and thus the Joker in the deck of cards. Stated more philosophically, each one of us is a manifestation of the total energy of the universe. Wearing clothes is therefore a gesture which implies the unadmitted knowledge that our personalities are put on. Think of such phrases as "cover yourself," "pull yourself together," "tighten your belts," "keep your hair on," "don't lose your shirt," "caught with your pants down," "shiftless," "sound investment," "redressment of injustice," "defrocked," "uncloaked," "dismantled," "name and address," "wearing an expression," "clothed and in one's right mind," "vested interest," "stuffed shirt," "good (or bad) habits," "the bare facts," and "the naked truth." Such a list of sartorial symbols and millinery metaphors for mental and moral states, of depletions and completions of personality, might be expanded indefinitely. But they express a basic and intuitive recognition of the connection between who we are, as persons, and what we wear.

Thus, may it not be significant that men who are supposed to play brahminical or "holy" roles in life wear loose-fitting robes—saddhus, swamis, monks, priests, professors in formal dress, and even judges? Very far-out holy men, such as the Shaiva yogis of India, go stark naked, to symbolize the supposition that they aren't playing any role at all, that they have entirely transcended the ego and reidentified with the divine. On the other hand, the aggressive, rough-and-tough military and business people are invariably trussed in armor, boots, puttees, Sam Brown belts, tight leather jackets, helmets, and other crustacean, squeeze-play contraptions for letting yourself know that you really exist. Yet again, the true athlete, like the far-out holy man, goes almost naked. The Greek word *gymnos* means "nude," and thus a gymnasium originally was a place where everyone took off their clothes for exercise.

These remarks must not suggest that I approve of nudism as a way of life. "Familiarity breeds contempt"—which is why something has to be done to reform the institution of the family—and "variety is the spice of life." The naked body is lustfully arousing, as it should be, just to the extent that it is usually veiled. Nudity must always be a revelation and a surprise for the simple reason that the universe itself is an energy system which vibrates: constantly it goes on and off. Now you see it; now you don't. It creeps up on itself and shouts "Boo!"—and then laughs at itself for jumping, being a constant conversion of anxiety into laughter, dread into delight, and hatred into love. Human consciousness is the realization that this is the case, is the nature of reality, which is why it is said throughout Asia that it is only from the human state that one can become a Buddha—a fully liberated being. (There are said to be five other states: happy angels, raging angels, animals, beings in hot and cold purgatories, and frustrated spirits with immense hungry bellies and mouths only as wide as needles. These are, of course, metaphors for our own changing states of mind.)

Energy going on and off may be represented, mythologically, as God playing hide-and-seek with himself, remembering himself and then dismembering himself into the myriad roles played by all sentient beings. That these roles are clothes is suggested in the *Bhagavad-Gita*, the summary of Hindu philosophy, versified by Sir Edwin Arnold in *The Song Celestial*:

> It is as when one layeth
>   His worn-out robes away,
> And, taking new ones, sayeth,
>   "These will I wear today."

So, according to Vedanta, the central doctrine of Hinduism, all bodies are the clothes of the one and only Self in its innumerable disguises, and the whole universe is a masquerade ball pretending to be a tragedy and then realizing that it's a ball.

Let's give away the secret that before God said, "Let there be light," he said, first, "You must draw the line somewhere," and, second, "Have a ball!"—which is why almost all heavenly bodies (including the earth) are spherical or cyclic. Energy not only goes on and off: it also balls. "It's love that makes the world go *round*."

It follows, then, that tight-fitting clothes are the opposite of masquerade. They represent the illusion that life is truly tragic and serious—that, in short, it is your sacred duty to survive. (And *sacer*, in Latin, means both "holy" and "accursed.") Life, like getting an erection, is a spontaneous process which collapses when one tries to force it to happen. The virile member wilts when *commanded* to be stiff. Uptight, militaristic clothing, and all the attitudes that go with it, are therefore comparable to a wimpus, or penile splint, such as employed by aged and impotent gentlemen who appreciate the joke that the four saddest words in the world are "Is it in yet?" This is natural enough in old gentlemen, and I do not wish to make fun of them, but it is destructive and deadly in those young and unrealized homosexuals who affect *machismo* (ultramasculinity) and who constitute the hard core of our military-industrial-police-mafia combine. If they would go and fuck each other (and I use that word in its most positive and appreciative sense), the world would be vastly improved. They make it with women only to brag about it, but are actually far happier in barracks than in boudoirs. This is, perhaps, the real meaning of the slogan "Make love, not war." We may be destroying ourselves through the repression of homosexuality.

Clothes, then, like our roles and personalities, should be worn easily and lightly in the realization that, because the whole universe is a masquerade, we may as well do it with the utmost flair and elegance. It is, I think, no secret that many women are sensually aroused by men in robes, because the robe—be it kimono, sarong, kaftan, or soutane—suggests that the man may really have something to conceal, whereas tight pants suggest that he does not. Furthermore, why not be comfortable—and even colorful? Why the self-humiliation and cryptomasochism of being ashamed to dress up? Because one must not be conspicuous in a democracy? Because one must go along with the modest mediocrity of one's academic, professional, or business colleagues? Because it implies that you have been so scurrilous as to make more money than the others? As fashion, among women, is the game of conforming faster than anyone else, so, among men, it is the game of "I am more modest and mature than you."

But, obviously, such games involve taking the ego and personality as a serious reality. They are very definitely uptight and stodgy. But if you *know* you are a fraud from the beginning, you can afford to be exuberant and flamboyant, and in any case, colorful and comfortable dress is a function of imagination rather than money.

When I am at home in California I usually wear a Japanese kimono around the house, or its more colorful version, the light

cotton *yukata*. But, in the United States, I don't yet have quite
the nerve to wear this attire on the streets. In San Francisco or
Los Angeles I can get away with Mexican Indian or Guate-
malan outfits, including those exquisite and cuddly woolen
jackets from Toluca, but in Chicago or New York I feel constrained to wear the conventional business suit on the principle
that "when in Rome, do as Rome does." Even so, I insist upon
sandals rather than shoes, for reasons already stated.

Some years ago a Japanese friend told me that he would no
longer even dream of wearing a kimono on the streets of Kyoto
because "You can't run for a bus in a kimono." True, but no
self-respecting person should ever run for a bus. However, you
certainly *can* run for a bus in a Philippine sarong, which is the
most comfortable male garment ever conceived—an ample divided skirt made of cotton batik, which could just as well be
silk or worsted, or even vicuña, plus, say, a vicuña poncho.

This sarong is a cylinder of cloth which, when laid out flat,
is about three feet wide and four feet long and, at the lower end,
is divided into two "legs" with a split of about two feet. You
step into it, adjust it to your waist-ankle length, and fold the
excess material (from the waist) inside. You then tighten it
around your waist, tuck in the overplus to the right, and secure
it with a safety pin. All in all you need two yards of material
some fifty inches wide. No belt, no zippers, no buttons, no
weirdities of tailoring. Above, you wear some attractive shirt
and a poncho for cold weather or rain. You are both comfortable and dignified. As for the nuisance of pockets, you take a
lesson from the Buddhist monks of South Asia, and wear a rectangular bag over your shoulder or around your neck, which is
secured by a short stole some three inches wide. If your belly
is of such proportions that you have no waist, you secure the

sarong with two strips of cloth going over the shoulders and crossing at the back so as not to slide off.

As for women, the incomparably comfortable and gracious garment is the sari. It suits all figures and comes in innumerable colors and designs. It makes you look like a queen, and you can pack twenty of them into a small suitcase, thus being able to change disguises three or four times a day. It is a simple rectangle of material six yards long and four feet wide, pleated around the waist, with a more highly ornamented end which is thrown over the left shoulder and secured with a brooch. It is worn with a skin-fitting blouse of complementary coloring. Furthermore, the manufacture of millions of saris for Western ladies would do wonders for the economies of India and Ceylon. And, since we are becoming accustomed to toplessness, suitably endowed girls might well be getting up the nerve to wear sarongs in the style of the Balinese, who go naked or elaborately necklaced from the waist up. Our homes are sufficiently heated that we can wear such garments even in winter, and one would merely have to don a fur or sheepskin coat to go out of doors.

I am commending Oriental and "primitive" styles of clothing not only because this would fulfill our obligation to boost the industry of the Third World, but also because it is all too true that "clothes make the man," and that our essentially military style of vesture may not be unconnected with our imperious and discourteous attitude toward other cultures, and our competitive and uptight relations among ourselves. Human beings the whole world over need to relax, become *gentle*men, take themselves lightly, and "come off it." Easy, gracious, and colorful clothing might well be a beginning.

THE SPIRIT OF VIOLENCE
AND THE MATTER OF PEACE

The idea that man has an instinct for violence must be questioned. Instincts, whether for violence, survival, reproduction, or food, would seem to be causes or explanations of the same type as humors, demons, or "acts of God"—that is to say, mythical agents or starters for processes that we do not fully understand, like the mysterious "it" in "it is raining." It is of great interest that many behavioral scientists now prefer to speak of *drives* rather than instincts, implying that when people feel angry, hungry, or lusty they feel like puppets, driven by forces beyond themselves. But this implies that "myself" is something less than my whole body and all its processes—a notion which I find absurd, however much it may correspond to our normal, but socially conditioned, ways of thinking and feeling.

Almost all civilized peoples have been brought up to think of themselves as ghosts in machines, as Koestler put it: as souls or spirits in alien bodies, as skin-encapsulated egos, or as psychic chauffeurs in mechanical vehicles of flesh and bone. We have learned to identify ourselves exclusively with that part of the brain which functions as a sort of radar or scanning apparatus and which is the apparent center of conscious attention and voluntary action. Although this center feels responsible for deliberate thinking, walking, talking, and handling, it knows next to nothing of *how* it manages to accomplish these actions. Furthermore, it experiences all the so-called involuntary functions of the body as events which simply happen to it. Thus it feels driven and passive with respect to strong emotions, to the circulation of the blood, and to the secretion of adrenalin.

There are those who feel that this separation of ego from body is the distinctively human achievement. They feel that it enables us, within certain limits, to subject nature to reason and to control what "merely happens" by the disciplines of art and science; and that it enables us to stand aside from ourselves and be critical of our own behavior, in short, to be self-conscious. Above all, it is supposed to be that unique function which "raises us above the animals," a boast which is beginning to sound increasingly hollow, since no mere animal seems to be preparing to destroy the planet as a by-product of war against its own species.

My home is at present a large boat in a quiet harbor where we are surrounded with birds—wild duck, grebes, pelicans, terns, and gulls galore. The latter are so ravenously hungry that they sometimes appear to me to be winged tubes with internal organs like a vacuum cleaner. Why do I feel that this world of birds is in some way more sane than the world of people? It must be hard work to be a bird, having to process enormous quantities of food through those short intestines. From the way gulls scramble and jostle each other for bits of bread, you would imagine that a single gull would be most happy to eat alone. But if you throw a crust to a lonely gull, it calls in a way that brings every other gull within hearing to the spot. Perhaps it doesn't know how to calculate, or just doesn't know how to restrain its squawks of delight. Maybe it isn't really an individual, but simply the subordinate organ of a gull-group something like a communist. Men have an envy of animals so deep that they will use any and every reason (the contradictions be damned) for proving their inferiority.

The root of this envy is the belief that animals, and especially free-flying birds, have no sense of responsibility. They hunt, nest, and breed without calculation, just as we breathe, hear, and grow hair. They "take no thought for the morrow," whereas self-conscious and self-critical man, with his sense of being in at least partial control of his actions, lies awake at night trying to make up his mind about important decisions or chiding himself for past mistakes. The individual human being is perpetually at odds with himself for not being sufficiently thoughtful, decisive, and self-controlled, regarding himself as civilized to the degree in which he manages to press this inner conflict to victory for the rational ego. Civilization is therefore attained through man's violence against himself—reflected in the flogging of his children, dogs, and horses, and in the brutal or subtle tortures inflicted upon those less successful and less cunning groups of bandits known as criminals. More and more, the scientists are saying that man must now take his future evolution into his own (i.e., the ego's) hands, and rely no longer upon the caprices of "natural selection." Yet those who speak thus do not seem to realize that this is going to require increasing violence against "deviant" forces within the individual and within society. The aspiration to direct evolution is also the aspiration to be "as God," and thus—as God is generally conceived in the West—to be dictator of the world.

But, as the psalm says, "Behold, He that keepeth Israel shall neither slumber nor sleep." This is really the same as the saying that "There is no peace for the wicked," for those who, like the tyrant-image of God, take the law into their own hands. For our traditional model of the universe is basically military.

> God, the all-terrible King,
>> Who ordainest
> Great winds Thy clarion
> And lightnings Thy sword.

This notion of the imperious violence of intelligent spirit against intractable and mindless matter is man's projection upon the universe of his own internal split, which is what keeps him awake at night worrying about his decisions—along with "He who keepeth Israel."

The basic problem is, of course, that law and reason are linear systems expressed in verbal, mathematical, or other forms of notation, of symbols strung out in a line to represent "bits" of information selected by the narrow spotlight of conscious attention. The physical world, by contrast, is at any moment a manifestation of innumerable and simultaneous energy patterns which, when we try to translate them into our clumsy linear symbols, seem impossibly complex. Actually, the world is not complex. It is the task of trying to figure it out with words or numbers which is complex; it is like trying to keep count of all the leaves in a constantly changing forest, or measuring the Atlantic with a hypodermic needle.

Nature can be "figured out" up to a certain indeterminate point, if we proceed patiently and humbly. But if at any time we decide that we actually know "the Truth," what the law of nature is, and therefore what is the right course of action, we shall find ourselves in the paradoxical situation of having to compel nature to submit to what we conceive to be its own laws!

As we say, "Dammit, why can't you be natural!" In other words, it is only by violence that the actual course of human and other physical events can be made to fit the oversimplified patterns in terms of which we attempt to describe it. We are like Procrustes, who stretched or amputated visitors to fit his guest-room bed.

We are working, then, on the (often tacit) assumption that the rational ego is a stranger and invader in the physical world, representing a conceptual and ideational order in necessary conflict with the chaotic complexity of nature. But when this supernaturalist assumption is brought out into the open it is hardly credible, since we also believe, at least in theory, that consciousness and intelligence arise through spontaneous evolution and are manifested through neural organizations which, as yet, we hardly understand.

This may be a "leap of faith," but I feel that if I am to trust myself I must bet on my entire nervous system (and the environment which, inseparably, goes with it) as distinct from a logic of words and numbers considered as something superior to its own neural matrix. For my brain is immeasurably more omniscient than my mind: it coordinates simultaneously more variables, more rhythms and patterns of bodily behavior, than I (as ego) could possibly comprehend in a hundred years of study. I can see no sense in restricting the definition of "myself" to the process of conscious attention, volition, and symbolization. I must admit my whole body to the definition of "myself," and so, in a certain way, assume responsibility for all that it is and does. After all, if I do not trust the matrix of my conscious intelligence, I have no assurance that this very mistrust is either well founded or well informed.

When Westerners contemplate their own bodies they are

apt to feel, with the psalmist, that they are "fearfully and won-derfully *made*"—that some agency and intelligence quite apart from themselves manufactured this intricate machine, which, in the same breath, they will "put down" as natural chaos or merely animal functioning. Thus to identify oneself with one's whole body is seen, ambivalently, both as blasphemy and as surrender to the blind forces of the unconscious. Whatever our metaphysics, we insist that inner conflict between ego and body, reason and instinct, is the essential condition of civilized life. But this attitude is penny-wise pound-foolish, for when we look at the trend of civilization as a whole we see a monstrous plague of human locusts devouring and fouling the planet, more preda-tory than sharks and more suicidal than lemmings. Civilization "works," temporarily, for the privileged individual, but in the not-so-long run it could easily be a speeding up of consumption which dissolves all life on the planet.

There is no question or possibility of abandoning technol-ogy and retreating into simple and sentimental anarchy. What we really need is a technology managed by people who no longer experience "self" as something foreign to the body and its physical environment. For it is precisely this interior con-flict between ego and organism which underlies organized warfare and violent revolution, most especially when such vi-olence is rationalized as being in the cause of justice and human betterment. No wars have been more ruthless and ravaging than "just" wars, fought in "defense" of religion, honor, or principle. If war must be, give me rather a war to capture an enemy's wealth and territory, based on honest greed, in which I shall be careful not to destroy what I want to possess. But as civilized wars are fought for principle, so the technologi-cal "conquest of nature" is in fact being waged for the purely abstract satisfaction of making money, as distinct from the material and sensuous enjoyment of good food, beautiful women, and elegant surroundings. Our greatest money makers are largely puritans and nose-to-the-grindstone people who have neither taste nor time for material pleasures. We need a technology aimed, not at abstract and inedible dollars, but at caviar and excellent wines the whole world round.

Only a supernaturalist would deliberately press the button to set off nuclear warfare, in the belief that his spiritual values are more important than material existence. And this involves the open or tacit supposition that the spiritual dimension is immortal, that in heaven or on some higher level of vibration unaffected by bodily death he will continue his existence, congratulating himself on his fidelity to principle and wagging the finger of reproof at the surprisedly immortal souls of dialectical materialists, eating crow in the sky instead of pie. This simply goes to show that belief in the superiority and final authority of the rational, intellectual, conceptual, and symbolic domain as the ultimate reality may be inconsistent with the survival of mankind.

Unexpectedly, naturalism is more consistent with the mystical vision of the world than supernaturalism, as should be clear from the suspicion in which mystics have always been held by the official establishments of Judaism, Christianity, and Islam. Supernaturalism splits the cosmos into the unequal duality of creator and creature, spirit and matter, ruler and subject, ego and organism, and many an atheist is in fact a supernaturalist insofar as he is trying to regulate the physical order of nature by the logical order of language or mathematics. But a naturalist cannot consistently subscribe to the belief that he himself is in any way separate from his whole physical organism. He cannot, therefore, consider himself driven or victimized by his own organic processes, for his emotions and appetites, and, indeed, the entire functioning of his body are his own doing, however spontaneous and undeliberate.

Once this is admitted, a further and essentially mystical insight comes into view. If I am my organism, I am also my environment. From the ecological and biophysical standpoints every organism goes with its environment transactionally: the one implies the other as buying implies selling and front implies back and the positive pole implies the negative. Thus every living organism implies, not only the conditions of the immediate solar system, but also the entire constellation of galaxies. If a human body could be transported to another universe, careful study by the local scientists would eventually reveal that it came from an environment which included sun, moon, planets, Milky Way, and the nebula in Andromeda. For as the fruit implies the tree, the human organism implies a cosmic energy system which "peoples" in the same way as a plant flowers.

Basically, then, "self" is not only the body but the whole energy system which embodies itself in all bodies. The conceptual ego does not control this system any more than it controls the heart, but whereas the ego is your idea of yourself, the total energy system of the universe is what you are. People who realize this could be trusted with technological power, for they would respect the external world, with all its subtle ecological balances, as they respect their own bodies. They would work with it and not against it, as a sailor works with the wind even when moving in a contrary direction.

The basic point to be understood, then, is that it is simply impossible to improve either oneself or the world by force.

Because you yourself *are* both the organism and its environment, this is as futile as trying to lift yourself off the floor by your own bootstraps. Untold psychic and physical energy is wasted in this ludicrous enterprise, which, when seen to be absurd, is abandoned, releasing that energy for tasks which can indeed be accomplished. Trying to force a lock bends the key, for which reason a truly intelligent man never forces an issue. He resorts instead to *judo*, the "gentle way" of trimming one's sails to the wind, of rolling with the punch, and of splitting wood along the grain. Such intelligence is therefore the alternative to violence.

PSYCHEDELICS AND RELIGIOUS EXPERIENCE

The experiences resulting from the use of psychedelic drugs are often described in religious terms. They are therefore of interest to those like myself who, in the tradition of William James, are concerned with the psychology of religion. For more than thirty years I have been studying the causes, consequences, and conditions of those peculiar states of consciousness in which the individual discovers himself to be one continuous process with God, with the Universe, with the Ground of Being, or whatever name he may use by cultural conditioning or personal preference for the ultimate and eternal reality. We have no satisfactory and definitive name for experiences of this kind. The terms "religious experience," "mystical experience," and "cosmic consciousness" are all too vague and comprehensive to denote that specific mode of consciousness which, to those who have known it, is as real and overwhelming as falling in love. This article describes such states of consciousness as and when induced by psychedelic drugs, although they are virtually indistinguishable from genuine mystical experience. It then discusses objections to the use of psychedelic drugs which arise mainly from the opposition between mystical values and the traditional religious and secular values of Western society.

I. THE PSYCHEDELIC EXPERIENCE

The idea of mystical experiences resulting from drug use is not readily accepted in Western societies. Western culture has, historically, a particular fascination with the value and virtue of man as an individual, self-determining, responsible ego, controlling himself and his world by the power of conscious effort and will. Nothing, then, could be more repugnant to this cultural tradition than the notion of spiritual or psychological growth through the use of drugs. A "drugged" person is by definition dimmed in consciousness, fogged in judgment, and deprived of will. But not all psychotropic (consciousness-changing) chemicals are narcotic and soporific, as are alcohol, opiates, and barbiturates. The effects of what are now called psychedelic (mind-manifesting) chemicals differ from those of alcohol as laughter differs from rage or delight from depression. There is really no analogy between being "high" on LSD and "drunk" on bourbon. True, no one in either state should drive a car, but neither should one drive while reading a book, playing a violin, or making love. Certain creative activities and states of mind demand a concentration and devotion which are simply incompatible with piloting a death-dealing engine along a highway.

I myself have experimented with five of the principal psychedelics: LSD-25, mescaline, psilocybin, dimethyltryptamine (DMT), and cannabis. I have done so, as William James tried nitrous oxide, to see if they could help me in identifying what might be called the "essential" or "active" ingredients of the mystical experience. For almost all the classical literature on mysticism is vague, not only in describing the experience, but also in showing rational connections between the experience itself and the various traditional methods recommended to induce it—fasting, concentration, breathing exercises, prayers, incantations, and dances. A traditional master of Zen or Yoga, when asked why such-and-such practices lead or predispose one to the mystical experience, always responds, "This is the way my teacher gave it to me. This is the way I found out. If you're seriously interested, try it for yourself." This answer hardly satisfies an impertinent, scientific-minded, and intellectually curious Westerner. It reminds him of archaic medical prescriptions compounding five salamanders, powdered gallowsrope, three boiled bats, a scruple of phosphorus, three pinches of henbane, and a dollop of dragon dung dropped when the moon was in Pisces. Maybe it worked, but what was the essential ingredient?

It struck me, therefore, that if any of the psychedelic chemicals would in fact predispose my consciousness to the mystical experience, I could use them as instruments for studying and describing that experience as one uses a microscope for bacteriology, even though the microscope is an "artificial" and "unnatural" contrivance which might be said to "distort" the vision of the naked eye. However, when I was first invited to test the mystical qualities of LSD-25 by Dr. Keith Ditman of the Neuropsychiatric Clinic at UCLA Medical School, I was unwilling to believe that any mere chemical could induce a genuine mystical experience. I though it might at most bring about a state of spiritual insight analogous to swimming with water wings. Indeed, my first experiment with LSD-25 was not mystical. It was an intensely interesting aesthetic and intellectual experience which challenged my powers of analysis and careful description to the utmost.

Some months later, in 1959, I tried LSD-25 again with Drs. Sterling Bunnell and Michael Agron, who were then associated with the Langley-Porter Clinic in San Francisco. In the course of two experiments I was amazed and somewhat embarrassed to find myself going through states of consciousness which corresponded precisely with every description of major mystical experiences I had ever read.[1] Furthermore, they exceeded both in depth and in a peculiar quality of unexpectedness the three "natural and spontaneous" experiences of this kind which I had had in previous years.

Through subsequent experimentation with LSD-25 and the other chemicals named above (with the exception of DMT, which I find amusing but relatively uninteresting) I found I could move with ease into the state of "cosmic consciousness," and in due course became less and less dependent on the chemicals themselves for "tuning in" to this particular wave-length of experience. Of the five psychedelics tried, I found that LSD-25 and cannabis suited my purposes best. Of these two, the latter, which I had to use abroad in countries where it is not outlawed, proved to be the better. It does not induce bizarre alterations of sensory perception, and medical studies indicate that it may not, save in great excess, have the dangerous side effects of LSD, such as psychotic episodes.

For the purposes of this study, in describing my experiences with psychedelic drugs, I avoid the occasional and incidental bizarre alterations of sense perception which psychedelic chemicals may induce. I am concerned, rather, with the fundamental alterations of the normal, socially induced consciousness of one's own existence and relation to the external world. I am trying to delineate the basic principles of psychedelic awareness. But I must add that I can speak only for myself. The quality of these experiences depends considerably upon one's prior

---

1 An excellent anthology of such experiences is Raynor C. Johnson, *Watcher on the Hills* (New York, Harper & Bros., 1959).

orientation and attitude to life, although the now voluminous descriptive literature of these experiences accords quite remarkably with my own.

Almost invariably, my experiments with psychedelics have had four dominant characteristics. I shall try to explain them— in the expectation that the reader will say, at least of the second and third, "Why, that's obvious! No one needs a drug to see that." Quite so, but every insight has degrees of intensity. There can be obvious$_1$ and obvious$_2$—and the latter comes on with shattering clarity, manifesting its implications in every sphere and dimension of our existence.

The first characteristic is a slowing down of time, a *concentration in the present*. One's normally compulsive concern for the future decreases, and one becomes aware of the enormous importance and interest of what is happening at the moment. Other people, going about their business on the streets, seem to be slightly crazy, failing to realize that the whole point of life is to be fully aware of it as it happens. One therefore relaxes, almost luxuriously, in studying the colors in a glass of water, or in listening to the now highly articulate vibration of every note played on an oboe or sung by voice.

From the pragmatic standpoint of our culture, such an attitude is very bad for business. It might lead to improvidence, lack of foresight, diminished sales of insurance policies, and abandoned savings accounts. Yet this is just the corrective that our culture needs. No one is more fatuously impractical than the "successful" executive who spends his whole life absorbed in frantic paperwork with the objective of retiring in comfort at sixty-five, when it will be all too late. Only those who have cultivated the art of living completely in the present have any use for making plans for the future, for when the plans mature they will be able to enjoy the results. "Tomorrow never comes." I have never yet heard a preacher urging his congregation to practice that section of the Sermon on the Mount which begins, "Be not anxious for the morrow...." The truth is that people who live for the future are, as we say of the insane, "not quite all there"—or here: by overeagerness they are perpetually missing the point. Foresight is bought at the price of anxiety, and, when overused, it destroys all its own advantages.

The second characteristic I will call *awareness of polarity*. This is the vivid realization that states, things, and events which we ordinarily call opposite are interdependent, like back and front or the poles of a magnet. By polar awareness one sees that things which are explicitly different are implicitly one: self and other, subject and object, left and right, male and female—and then, a little more surprisingly, solid and space, figure and background, pulse and interval, saints and sinners, and police and criminals, ingroups and outgroups. Each is definable only in terms of the other, and they go together transactionally, like buying and selling, for there is no sale without a purchase, and no purchase without a sale. As this awareness becomes increasingly intense, you feel that you yourself are polarized with the external universe in such a way that you imply each other. Your push is its pull, and its push is your pull—as when you move the steering wheel of a car. Are you pushing it or pulling it?

At first, this is a very odd sensation, not unlike hearing your own voice played back to you on an electronic system immediately after you have spoken. You become confused, and wait for *it* to go on! Similarly, you feel that you are something being done by the universe, yet that the universe is equally something being done by you—which is true, at least in the neurological sense that the peculiar structure of our brains translates the sun into light and air vibrations into sound. Our normal sensation of relationship to the outside world is that sometimes we push it, and sometimes it pushes us. But if the two are actually one, where does action begin and responsibility rest? If the universe is doing me, how can I be sure that, two seconds hence, I will still remember the English language? If I am doing it, how can I be sure that, two seconds hence, my brain will know how to turn the sun into light? From such unfamiliar sensations as these the psychedelic experience can generate confusion, paranoia, and terror—even though the individual is feeling his relationship to the world exactly as it would be described by a biologist, ecologist, or physicist, for he is feeling himself as the unified field of organism and environment.

The third characteristic, arising from the second, is *awareness of relativity*. I see that I am a link in an infinite hierarchy of processes and beings, ranging from molecules through bacteria and insects to human beings, and, maybe, to angels and gods—a hierarchy in which every level is in effect the same situation. For example, the poor man worries about money while the rich man worries about his health: the worry is the same, but the difference is in its substance or dimension. I realize that fruit flies must think of themselves as people, because, like ourselves, they find themselves in the middle of their own world—with immeasurably greater things above and smaller things below. To us, they all look alike and seem to have no personality—as do the Chinese when we have not lived among them. Yet fruit flies must see just as many subtle distinctions among themselves as we among ourselves.

From this it is but a short step to the realization that all forms of life and being are simply variations on a single theme: we are all in fact one being doing the same thing in as many different ways as possible. As the French proverb goes, *plus ça*

change, plus c'est la même chose—"the more it varies, the more
it is one." I see, further, that feeling threatened by the in-
evitability of death is really the same experience as feeling alive,
and that as all beings are feeling this everywhere, they are all
just as much "I" as myself. Yet the "I" feeling, to be felt at
all, must always be a sensation relative to the "other," to something beyond its control and experience. To be at all, it must
begin and end. But the intellectual jump which mystical and
psychedelic experience make here is in enabling you to see that
all these myriad I-centers are yourself—not, indeed, your personal and superficial conscious ego, but what Hindus call the
paramatman, the Self of all selves.[2] As the retina enables us to
see countless pulses of energy as a single light, so the mystical
experience shows us innumerable individuals as a single Self.

The fourth characteristic is *awareness of eternal energy*, often
in the form of intense white light, which seems to be both the
current in your nerves and that mysterious *e* which equals mc^2.
This may sound like megalomania or delusion of grandeur—
but one sees quite clearly that all existence is a single energy,
and that this energy is one's own being. Of course there is death
as well as life, because energy is a pulsation, and just as waves
must have both crests and troughs, the experience of existing

---

2 Thus Hinduism regards the universe, not as an artifact, but as an immense drama
  in which the One Actor (the *paramatman* or *brahman*) plays all the parts, which
  are his (or "its") masks, or *personae*. The sensation of being only this one particular self, John Doe, is due to the Actor's total absorption in playing this and
  every other part. For fuller exposition, see Sarvepalli Radhakrishnan, *The Hindu
  View of Life* (New York, The Macmillan Company, 1927); Heinrich Zimmer,
  Philosophies of India (New York, Pantheon Books, 1951), pp. 355–463. A popular version is in Alan Watts, *The Book: On the Taboo Against Knowing Who You
  Are* (New York, Pantheon Books, 1966).

must go on and off. Basically, therefore, there is simply nothing to worry about, because you yourself are the eternal energy of the universe playing hide-and-seek (off-and-on) with itself. At root, you are the Godhead, for God is all that there is. Quoting Isaiah just a little out of context: "I am the Lord, and there is none else. I form the light and create the darkness: I make peace, and create evil. I, the Lord, do all these things."[3] This is the sense of the fundamental tenet of Hinduism, *Tat tvam asi*—"THAT (i.e., 'that subtle Being of which this whole universe is composed') art thou."[4] A classical case of this experience, from the West, is described by Tennyson:

> A kind of waking trance I have frequently had, quite up from boyhood, when I have been all alone. This has generally come upon me thro' repeating my own name two or three times to myself silently, till all at once, as it were out of the intensity of the consciousness of individuality, the individuality itself seemed to dissolve and fade away into boundless being, and this is not a confused state, but the clearest of the clearest, the surest of the surest, the weirdest of the weirdest, utterly beyond words, where death was an almost laughable impossibility, the loss of personality (if so it were) seeming no extinction but the only true life.[5]

Obviously, these characteristics of the psychedelic experience, as I have known it, are aspects of a single state of consciousness—for I have been describing the same thing from

---

3 *Isaiah*, 45: 6, 7.
4 *Chandogya Upanishad* 6.15.3.
5 *Alfred Lord Tennyson, A Memoir by His Son* (1898), Vol. I, p. 320.

different angles. The descriptions attempt to convey the reality of the experience, but in doing so they also suggest some of the inconsistencies between such experience and the current values of society.

II. OPPOSITION TO PSYCHEDELIC DRUGS

Resistance to allowing use of psychedelic drugs originates in both religious and secular values. The difficulty in describing psychedelic experiences in traditional religious terms suggests one ground of opposition. The Westerner must borrow such words as *samadhi* or *moksha* from the Hindus, or *satori* or *kensho* from the Japanese, to describe the experience of oneness with the universe. We have no appropriate word because our own Jewish and Christian theologies will not accept the idea that man's inmost self can be identical with the Godhead, even though Christians may insist that this was true in the unique instance of Jesus Christ. Jews and Christians think of God in political and monarchical terms, as the supreme governor of the universe, the ultimate boss. Obviously, it is both socially unacceptable and logically preposterous for a particular individual to claim that he, in person, is the omnipotent and omniscient ruler of the world—to be accorded suitable recognition and honor.

Such an imperial and kingly concept of the ultimate reality, however, is neither necessary nor universal. The Hindus and the Chinese have no difficulty in conceiving of an identity of the self and the Godhead. For most Asians, other than Moslems, the Godhead moves and manifests the world in much the same way that a centipede manipulates a hundred legs: spontaneously, without deliberation or calculation. In other words, they conceive the universe by analogy with an organism as distinct from a mechanism. They do not see it as an artifact or construct under the conscious direction of some supreme technician, engineer, or architect.

If, however, in the context of Christian or Jewish tradition an individual declares himself to be one with God, he must be dubbed blasphemous (subversive) or insane. Such a mystical experience is a clear threat to traditional religious concepts. The Judaeo-Christian tradition has a monarchical image of God, and monarchs, who rule by force, fear nothing more than insubordination. The Church has therefore always been highly suspicious of mystics because they seem to be insubordinate and to claim equality or, worse, identity with God. For this reason John Scotus Erigena and Meister Eckhart were condemned as heretics. This was also why the Quakers faced opposition for their doctrine of the Inward Light, and for their refusal to remove hats in church and in court. A few occasional mystics may be all right so long as they watch their language, like Saint Teresa of Avila and Saint John of the Cross, who maintained, shall we say, a metaphysical distance of respect between themselves and their heavenly King. Nothing, however, could be more alarming to the ecclesiastical hierarchy than a popular outbreak of mysticism, for this might well amount to setting up a democracy in the kingdom of heaven—and such alarm would be shared equally by Catholics, Jews, and fundamentalist Protestants.

The monarchical image of God with its implicit distaste for religious insubordination has a more pervasive impact than many Christians might admit. The thrones of kings have walls immediately behind them, and all who present themselves at court must prostrate themselves or kneel because this is an awkward position from which to make a sudden attack. It has perhaps never occurred to Christians that when they design a church on the model of a royal court (basilica) and prescribe church ritual, they are implying that God, like a human monarch, is afraid. This is also implied by flattery in prayers:

> O Lord our heavenly Father, high and mighty, King of kings, Lord of lords, the only Ruler of princes, who dost from thy throne behold all the dwellers upon earth: most heartily we beseech thee with thy favor to behold . . .

The Western man who claims consciousness of oneness with God or the universe thus clashes with his society's concept of religion. In most Asian cultures, however, such a man will be congratulated as having penetrated the true secret of life. He has arrived, by chance or by some such discipline as Yoga or Zen meditation, at a state of consciousness in which he experiences directly and vividly what our own scientists know to be true in theory. For the ecologist, the biologist, and the physicist know (but seldom feel) that every organism constitutes a single field of behavior, or process, with its environment. There is no way of separating what any given organism is doing from what its environment is doing, for which reason ecologists speak not of organisms in environments but of organism-environments. Thus the words "I" or "self" should properly mean what the whole universe is doing at this particular "here-and-now" called John Doe.

The kingly concept of God makes identity of self and God, or self and universe, inconceivable in Western religious terms. The difference between Eastern and Western concepts of man and his universe, however, extends beyond strictly religious concepts. The Western scientist may rationally perceive the idea of organism-environment, but he does not ordinarily *feel* this to be true. By cultural and social conditioning, he has been hypnotized into experiencing himself as an ego—as an isolated center of consciousness and will inside a bag of skin, confronting an external and alien world. We say, "I came into this world." But we did nothing of the kind. We came *out* of it in just the same way that fruit comes out of trees. Our galaxy, our cosmos "peoples" in the same way that an apple tree "apples."

Such a vision of the universe clashes with the idea of a monarchical God, with the concept of the separate ego, and even with the secular, atheist-agnostic mentality, which derives its common sense from the mythology of nineteenth-century scientism. According to this view, the universe is a mindless mechanism and man a sort of accidental microorganism infesting a minute globular rock which revolves about an unimportant star on the outer fringe of one of the minor galaxies. This "putdown" theory of man is extremely common among such quasi-scientists as sociologists, psychologists, and psychiatrists, most of whom are still thinking of the world in terms of Newtonian mechanics, and have never really caught up with the ideas of Einstein and Bohr, Oppenheimer and Schrödinger. Thus to the ordinary institutional-type psychiatrist, any patient who gives the least hint of mystical or religious experience is automatically diagnosed as deranged. From the standpoint of the mechanistic religion he is a heretic and is given electroshock therapy as an up-to-date form of thumbscrew and rack. And, incidentally, it is just this kind of quasi-scientist who, as consultant to government and law-enforcement agencies, dictates official policies on the use of psychedelic chemicals.

Inability to accept the mystic experience is more than an intellectual handicap. Lack of awareness of the basic unity of organism and environment is a serious and dangerous hallucination. For in a civilization equipped with immense technological power, the sense of alienation between man and nature leads to the use of technology in a hostile spirit—to the "conquest" of nature instead of intelligent cooperation with nature. The result is that we are eroding and destroying our environment, spreading Los Angelization instead of civilization. This is the major threat overhanging Western technological culture, and no amount of reasoning or doom-preaching seems to help. We simply do not respond to the prophetic and moralizing techniques of conversion upon which Jews and Christians have always relied. But people have an obscure sense of what is good for them—call it "unconscious self-healing," "survival instinct," "positive growth potential," or what you will. Among the educated young there is therefore a startling and unprecedented interest in the transformation of human consciousness. All over the Western world publishers are selling millions of books dealing with Yoga, Vedanta, Zen Buddhism, and the chemical mysticism of psychedelic drugs, and I have come to believe that the whole "hip" subculture, however misguided in some of its manifestations, is the earnest and responsible effort of young people to correct the self-destroying course of industrial civilization.

The content of the mystical experience is thus inconsistent with both the religious and secular concepts of traditional Western thought. Moreover, mystical experiences often result in attitudes which threaten the authority not only of established churches but also of secular society. Unafraid of death and deficient in worldly ambition, those who have undergone mystical experiences are impervious to threats and promises. Moreover, their sense of the relativity of good and evil arouses the suspicion that they lack both conscience and respect for law. Use of psychedelics in the United States by a literate bourgeoisie means that an important segment of the population is indifferent to society's traditional rewards and sanctions.

In theory, the existence within our secular society of a group which does not accept conventional values is consistent with our political vision. But one of the great problems of the United States, legally and politically, is that we have never quite had the courage of our convictions. The republic is founded on the marvelously sane principle that a human community can exist and prosper only on a basis of mutual trust. Metaphysically, the American Revolution was a rejection of the dogma of Original Sin, which is the notion that because you cannot trust yourself or other people, there must be some Superior Authority to keep us all in order. The dogma was rejected because if it is true that we cannot trust ourselves and others, it follows that we cannot trust the Superior Authority which we ourselves conceive and obey, and that the very idea of our own untrustworthiness is unreliable!

Citizens of the United States believe, or are supposed to believe, that a republic is the best form of government. Yet, vast confusion arises from trying to be republican in politics and monarchist in religion. How can a republic be the best form of government if the universe, heaven, and hell are a monarchy?[6] Thus, despite the theory of government by consent, based upon mutual trust, the peoples of the United States retain, from the

---

6 Thus, until quite recently, belief in a Supreme Being was a legal test of valid conscientious objection to military service. The implication was that the individual objector found himself bound to obey a higher echelon of command than the President and Congress. The analogy is military and monarchical, and therefore objectors who, as Buddhists or naturalists, held an organic theory of the universe often had difficulty in obtaining recognition.

authoritarian backgrounds of their religions or national origins, an utterly naive faith in law as some sort of supernatural and paternalistic power. "There ought to be a law against it!" Our law-enforcement officers are therefore confused, hindered, and bewildered—not to mention corrupted—by being asked to enforce sumptuary laws, often of ecclesiastical origin, which vast numbers of people have no intention of obeying and which, in any case, are immensely difficult or simply impossible to enforce—for example, the barring of anything so undetectable as LSD-25 from international and interstate commerce.

There are two specific objections to use of psychedelic drugs. First, use of these drugs may be dangerous. However, every worthwhile exploration is dangerous—climbing mountains, testing aircraft, rocketing into outer space, skin diving, or collecting botanical specimens in jungles. But if you value knowledge and the actual delight of exploration more than mere duration of uneventful life, you are willing to take the risks. It is not really healthy for monks to practice fasting, and it was hardly hygienic for Jesus to get himself crucified, but these are risks taken in the course of spiritual adventures. Today the adventurous young are taking risks in exploring the psyche, testing their mettle at the task just as, in times past, they have tested it—more violently—in hunting, dueling, hot-rod racing, and playing football. What they need is not prohibitions and policemen but the most intelligent encouragement and advice that can be found.

Second, drug use may be criticized as an escape from reality. However, this criticism assumes unjustly that the mystical experiences themselves are escapist or unreal. LSD, in particular, is by no means a soft and cushy escape from reality. It can very easily be an experience in which you have to test your soul against all the devils in hell. For me, it has been at times an experience in which I was at once completely lost in the corridors of the mind and yet relating that very lostness to the exact order of logic and language, simultaneously very mad and very sane. But beyond these occasional lost and insane episodes, there are the experiences of the world as a system of total harmony and glory, and the discipline of relating these to the order of logic and language must somehow explain how what William Blake called that "energy which is eternal delight" can coexist with the misery and suffering of everyday life.[7]

The undoubted mystical and religious intent of most users of the psychedelics, even if some of these substances should be proved injurious to physical health, requires that their free and responsible use be exempt from legal restraint in any republic which maintains a constitutional separation of Church and State. I mean "responsible" in the sense that such substances be taken by or administered to consenting adults only. The user of cannabis, in particular, is apt to have peculiar difficulties in establishing his "undoubtedly mystical and religious intent" in court. Having committed so loathsome and serious a felony, his chances of clemency are better if he assumes a repentant demeanor, which is quite inconsistent with the sincere belief that his use of cannabis was religious. On the other hand, if he insists unrepentantly that he looks upon such use as a religious

---

7 This is discussed at length in A. Watts, *The Joyous Cosmology: Adventures in the Chemistry of Consciousness* (New York: Pantheon Books, 1962).

sacrament, many judges will declare that they "dislike his attitude," finding it truculent and lacking in appreciation of the
gravity of the crime, and the sentence will be that much harsher.
The accused is therefore put in a "double-bind" situation in
which he is "damned if he does, and damned if he doesn't."
furthermore, religious integrity—as in conscientious objection—is generally tested and established by membership in
some church or religious organization with a substantial following. But the felonious status of cannabis is such that grave
suspicion would be cast upon all individuals forming such an
organization, and the test cannot therefore be fulfilled. It is
generally forgotten that our guarantees of religious freedom
were designed to protect precisely those who were *not* members of established denominations, but rather such screwball
and (then) subversive individuals as Quakers, Shakers, Lev-
ellers, and Ana-baptists. There is little question that those who
use cannabis, or other psychedelics, with religious intent are
now members of a persecuted religion which appears to the rest
of society as a grave menace to "mental health," as distinct from
the old-fashioned "immortal soul." But it's the same old story.

To the extent that mystical experience conforms with the
tradition of genuine religious involvement, and to the extent
that psychedelics induce that experience, users are entitled to
some constitutional protection. Also, to the extent that research
in the psychology of religion can utilize such drugs, students
of the human mind must be free to use them. Under present
laws, I, as an experienced student of the psychology of religion,
can no longer pursue research in the field. This is a barbarous
restriction of spiritual and intellectual freedom, suggesting
that the legal system of the United States, is, after all, in tacit

alliance with the monarchical theory of the universe and will, therefore, prohibit and persecute religious ideas and practices based on an organic and unitary vision of the universe.[8]

---

8 Amerindians belonging to the Native American Church, who employ the psychedelic peyote cactus in their rituals, are firmly opposed to any government control of this plant, even if they should be guaranteed the right to its use. They feel that peyote is a natural gift of God to mankind, and especially to natives of the land where it grows, and that no government has a right to interfere with its use. The same argument might be made on behalf of cannabis, or the mushroom *Psilocybe mexicana Heim.* All these things are natural plants, not processed or synthesized drugs, and by what authority can individuals be prevented from eating them? There is no law against eating or growing the mushroom *Amanita pantherina*, even though it is fatally poisonous and only experts can distinguish it from a common edible mushroom. This case can be made even from the standpoint of believers in the monarchical universe of Judaism and Christianity, for it is a basic principle of both religions, derived from Genesis, that all natural substances created by God are inherently good, and that evil can arise only in their misuse. Thus laws against mere possession, or even cultivation, of these plants are in basic conflict with Biblical principles. Criminal conviction of those who employ these plants should be based on proven misuse. "And God said, 'Behold, I have given you *every* herb bearing seed, which is upon the face of all the earth, and every tree, in which is the fruit of a tree yielding seed; to you it shall be for meat.' ... And God saw every thing that he had made, and, behold, it was very good." (Genesis 1:29, 31.)

SEVEN SHORT ESSAYS

THE BASIC MYTH

According to the Tradition of Ancient India

In the beginning—which was not long ago but now-ever—is the Self. Everyone knows the Self, but no one can describe it, just as the eye sees but does not see itself. Moreover, the Self is what there is and all that there is, so that no name can be given to it. It is neither old nor new, great nor small, shaped nor shapeless. Having no opposite, it is what all opposites have in common: it is the reason why there is no white without black and no form apart from emptiness. However, the Self has two sides, the inside and the outside. The inside is called *nirguna*, which is to say that it has no qualities and nothing can be said or thought about it. The outside is *saguna*, which is to say that it may be considered as eternal reality, consciousness, and delight. Thus the story which follows will be told of the *saguna* side.

Because of delight the Self is always at play, and its play, called *lila*, is like singing or dancing, which are made of sound and silence, motion and rest. Thus the play of the Self is to lose itself and to find itself in a game of hide-and-seek without beginning or end. In losing itself it is dismembered: it forgets that it is the one and only reality, and plays that it is the vast multitude of beings and things which make up this world. In finding itself it is remembered: it discovers again that it is forever the one behind the many, the trunk within the branches, that its seeming to be many is always *maya*, which is to say illusion, art, and magical power.

The playing of the Self is therefore like a drama in which the Self is both the actor and the audience. On entering the theater the audience knows that what it is about to see is only a play, but the skillful actor creates a *maya*, an illusion of reality which gives the audience delight or terror, laughter or tears. It is thus that in the joy and the sorrow of all beings the Self as audience is carried away by itself as actor.

One of the many images of the Self is the *hamsa*, the Divine Bird which lays the world in the form of an egg. It is said also that with the syllable *ham* the Self breathes out, scattering all galaxies into the sky, and that with the syllable *sa* it breathes in, withdrawing all things to their original unity. Yet if one repeats the syllables *ham-sa* they may also be heard as *sa-ham* or *sa-aham*, which is to say "I am that," or THAT (the Self) is what each and every being is. As breathing out, the Self is called Brahma, the creator. As holding the breath out, the Self is called Vishnu, the preserver of all these worlds. And as breathing in, the Self is called Shiva, the destroyer of illusion.

This is, then, a story without beginning or end since the Self breathes out and in, loses itself and finds itself, for always and always, and these periods are sometimes known as its days and nights—each day and each night lasting for a *kalpa*, which is 4,320,000 of our years. The day, or *manvantara*, is further divided into four *yuga*, or epochs, which are named after the throws in a game of dice: first *krita*, the perfect throw with a score of four; second *treta*, with a score of three; third *dvapara*, with a score of two; and fourth *kali*, the worst throw with a score of one.

Krita yuga is the Golden Age, the era of total delight in

multiplicity and form and every beauty of the sensuous world, enduring for 1,728,000 years. *Treta yuga* is somewhat shorter, lasting for 1,296,000 years, and is like an apple with a single maggot in the core: things have just started to go amiss and every pleasure contains a slight shadow of anxiety. *Dvapara yuga* is shorter still. Its time is 864,000 years, and now the forces of light and darkness, good and evil, pleasure and pain, are evenly balanced. In the temporary end there come the 432,000 years of the *kali yuga* when the world is overwhelmed by darkness and decay, and when the Self is so lost to itself that all its delight appears in the disguise of horror. Finally, the Self is manifested in the form of Shiva, ten-armed and blue-bodied and wreathed in fire, to dance the terrible *tandava*-dance whereby the universe, incandescent with his heat, turns to ash and nothingness. But as the illusion vanishes the Self finds itself in its original unity and bliss, and remains for another *kalpa* of 4,320,000 years in the *pralaya* of total peace before losing itself again.

The worlds that are manifested when the Self breathes out are not just this one here and those that we see in the sky, for besides these there are worlds so small that ten thousand of them may be hidden in the tip of a butterfly's tongue, and so large that all our stars may be contained in the eye of a shrimp. There are also worlds within and around us that do not reverberate upon our five organs of sense, and all these worlds, great and small, visible and invisible, are in number as many as grains of sand in the Ganges.

Throughout these manifested worlds all sentient beings pass through the six paths or divisions of the Wheel of Becoming. These, counting clockwise from the top of the Wheel, are, first, the realm of the *deva*, that is, of gods and angels at the summit of happiness and spiritual success. Second is the realm of the *ashura*, of dark angels who manifest the Self in the bliss of rage. Third is the realm of animals, of beasts, fish, birds, and insects. Fourth is the *naraka* realm, which is the depth of misery and spiritual failure, lying at the bottom of the Wheel and comprising the purgatories of ice and fire, manifesting the Self in the ecstasy of pain. Fifth is the realm of the *preta*, that is, of frustrated ghosts having immense bellies and tiny mouths. Sixth, and last, is the realm of mankind. All beings in the six paths are bound to the Wheel of Becoming by their *karma*, which is to say action motivated by desire for results—whether good or evil. Every being is desirous for the fruits of action so long as it remains ignorant of its true nature, thinking "I have come to be, and I shall cease to be," not realizing that there is no "I," no Self, except that which is one and original and beyond all time and space.

It is thus that anyone who, setting aside all ideas and theories, and looking earnestly and intently at the feeling of "I am," will—all of a sudden—awaken to the knowledge that there is no self but the Self. Such a one is called *jivanmukta*, that is, liberated while still in his individual form, before the death of the body, and before the dissolution of all worlds at the end of the *kalpa*. For him there is no longer self and other, mine and yours, success and failure. On all sides, within and without, he sees all beings, all things, all events, only as the playing of the Self in its myriad forms.

THE GREAT MANDALA

People have always been fascinated by circles of glory, known in India as *mandala*: the rose windows of gothic cathedrals, Byzantine mosaic upon the inner surface of a dome, the radiant and radiating petals of certain flowers, the design of snow crystals, precious stones set in coronas of varicolored gems, and *mandala* proper as they are found in Tibetan painting—circular paradise gardens with their jeweled plants and trees surrounding an inner circle of Dhyani Buddhas and their attendant Bodhisattvas. It is in this form, too, that Dante described his vision of God, ringed by the saints and angels, at the end of the *Paradiso*.

C. G. Jung suggested that this fascination might be explained by some correspondence between the *mandala* form and the basic formative energy of the psyche. For there is indeed an almost universal tendency to express the divine in terms of radiating light. Sometimes I wish I had the time and skill to project such an image in motion and in highly articulate form and color upon the dome of a planetarium, as in the Vortex demonstrations of Jacobs and Belsen.

I think of a sunburst of electric blue-white light lasting only long enough to avoid blinding the eyes, and then softening to white gold. With the light goes sound, the high, exulting blast of Gabriel's trumpet that shatters the sleep of the dead. The sunburst recedes (or ascends) to its own center, and as it does so gives out a concentric aureole of fluorescent red, and then, ring upon ring, the whole visual spectrum—orange, yellow, green, blue, indigo, purple—and beyond a transparent, mirrorlike blackness, about which a ring of lightning sets off another rainbow circle encompassing the first. And as the colored rings emerge, the sound descends at various harmonic intervals until, with the lacquer black, it reaches a bass so deep as to shake the walls and become tangible, thus generating a spectrum of vibrations that are felt only by the skin, converting the sonic into the solid, and all its textures.

In turn, these vibrations affect the mucous membrane of the nose, evoking a procession of scents which begins with *jinko*, or burning aloes wood, the perfume most pleasing to Buddha, and descending through roses, carnations, and the salt wind of the sea, to freshly ground coffee, mint, thyme, and warm brandy, and then on to excellent cheese, to ammonia, excrement, and burning blood.

The ordered rings and sequences of vibration touch every sense and emotion, and, as the lacquer black generates lightning, it becomes clear that feeling is a cycle in which the highest intensities of pleasure and pain are the same extreme.

But thus far the image has been only of rings and sequences. Within the rings we now distinguish rays, innumerable, but shooting straight as spokes from the central light. A moment later, the rays ripple, and with them the descending tones of sound begin to oscillate. Likewise the vibrations of scent, texture, and taste start to mix and combine according to an arithmetic that becomes increasingly complex. And the ripples are now something more than simple undulations: they are curves turning back upon themselves, spirals winding and unwinding, begetting patterns that resemble sunlit smoke, or foam in broken waves.

Soon this immense arabesque of curling forms develops sharp corners. The rays bend instantly and jump into angles, squares, diamonds, and frets. Simultaneously the other spectra—of sound, texture, taste, and smell—are moving in rhythms and patterns equivalently varied. But just as the dance of vibrations is about to blast the brain, there emerge the forms of ferns and fronds, of watercourses and trees, of ocean waves and mountains, of flowers and shells, of insects, fish, and human faces—all writhing and squirming within the total configuration of concentric rings.

Just then, one is aware that the whole scene has become three-dimensional: the flat circle is a globe, the sound is from every direction, and one is simply engulfed in the vibrations of texture and smell. In some way, the viewer is now *inside* the spectacle, and his sense of the total form diminishes because of the increasing interest of the detail—the articulation of particular features, of flowers and faces, gardens and cities, rivers and roads. As vision concentrates, the vibrations of sound, touch, smell, and taste become consistent with such details as fascinate the eye. And just then, before we know it, the spectacle as a whole is forgotten. Quite suddenly, we discover ourselves and our surroundings just as they are, here and now.

ON SELECTING VIBRATIONS

Are you yet ready to admit that what you will and what you won't are one and the same process? ... That as the recognition of a figure requires a background, the sense of being "oneself" requires the apprehension that there is something "other" and external, and that the achievement of any kind of power, success, or control cannot be experienced apart from a perpetual contract of failure, surprise, and unpredictability? ... That, therefore, all our pretentious projects for power over circumstance are a sort of joke or game which, if taken seriously, lead to mayhem and violence—expressing sheer rage at being unable to solve a problem which was absurd from the beginning?

If there is any meaning to the doctrine of Original Sin, transmitted from generation to generation from Adam and Eve, it is simply that all infants are brainwashed or hypnotized by their parents and teachers, elders and betters, into the notion that survival is a frantic necessity. They are taught, by adult reactions and attitudes, that certain experiences of high tension or vibration are to be regarded as "painful" and "bad" because they may be precursors of the monstrous event of death, which absolutely should not happen. Let me cite only two examples of this basic brainwashing to illustrate its fundamental principle—both of them down to what we are now calling the "nitty-gritty" level of things.

We now know that a woman giving birth to a baby does not have to go through "labor pains." She can be mentally re-oriented to experience what was formerly called pain as orgiastic tension, and therefore find the sensation of birth as erotically arousing as was the sensation of conception. Adults are wont to impress all infants with the vast importance of having regular bowel movements, but when the infant, with understandable pride, complies and does his production, the adults turn up their noses and complain of the stink. What on earth, he wonders, do these mysterious grownups really want?

They do not know. They have never thought it consistently through. The point, however, is that the cosmos is a complex, multidimensional system of vibrations arranged in crisscrossing spectra, as in weaving, and from these—as in playing a harp—we pluck and choose those that are to be considered valuable, important, or pleasant, ignoring or repressing those which (under the rules of our not always well-considered games) we deem unimportant or offensive. "Negative" experiences—which may include physical pain, death, vomiting, dizziness, or even sexual lust (according to taste)—are to be avoided, in the same way and sense that the rules of classical Western music excluded the augmented fourth (e.g., C to F sharp) as a permissible interval.

Liberation, in the Buddhist sense of *nirvana* or the Hindu of *moksha*, is the realization that ultimately, it doesn't really matter what strings are plucked or what vibrations occur. Thus a great yogi can face torture with equanimity for the very reason that he can *allow* himself to writhe and scream, and to dislike the experience immensely. He trusts his nature—that is, Nature itself—to do whatever is appropriate under the circumstances. He knows that energy always takes the line of least resistance, and that all motion is essentially gravity or falling. His basic commitment is therefore to what Ananda Coomaraswamy called "the perpetual uncalculated life in the present."

This, however, does not deny the value of culture, art, and morality. On the contrary, it is their essential basis in somewhat the same way that a clean, blank page is the essential basis for writing poetry. Every writer, every poet, loves white paper. As nature abhors a vacuum it sucks out one's creative energy, and this is why the *Heart Sutra* of Mahayana Buddhism asserts that emptiness (or void or space) is form, and that form is emptiness.

Now then, to see that we live in a universe where, basically, "anything goes" is what the Mahayana calls *prajna* or intuitive wisdom. But the inseparable handmaid of *prajna* is *karuna*, compassion, which is asking the question: "Given a universe in which anything goes, what are the most lovely, generous, and exuberant things we can do?" Why not ask the opposite question: "What are the most horrible and hateful deeds we can perpetrate?" The answer is irrational or perhaps supra-rational. It is that the whole system of vibration spectra, although comprising intensities of experience that we now call pure agony, is a celebration of love and delight which, were it otherwise, would simply not go on happening. The so-called instinct for survival, for going on and on because one *must*, is a parody of this celebration—undertaken by beings who doggedly believe themselves to be strangers in the cosmos and victims of its machinations. The beautiful task of a bodhisattva is precisely to deliver them from this belief.

If you get with yourself, get with gravity, get with energy (following its line of least resistance), you will discover that all the vibrations of nature are ecstatic, erotic, or blissful. Existence is orgasm. This is why the Vedanta philosophy terms the vibration-system *sat-chit-ananda*—reality-awareness-ecstasy. The naturally falling, simply and effortlessly given *you*, is Nature itself; it is not something trapped in the energy system of the world: it is that very system. Death does not abolish you; it is one term or end of the spectrum that *is* you. Energy cannot be stopped because energy is vibration, and vibration is exactly starting/stopping or on-and-off. Existence includes both being and nonbeing, solid and space, form and void.

Following the line of least resistance is, of course, easy; but it requires intelligence. It is not followed by imitating some preconceived notion of spontaneous behavior. Such imitations have been covering the walls of Western art galleries for thirty years, and many have affected spontaneity by copying forms of conduct *supposed* to be characteristic of animals. (Real animals, incidentally, have far higher standards of behavior than human beings. Consider the dolphins. And the sharks don't fly out of the water to eat us.)

Indeed, the flow patterns of water are a basic model for the conduct of life, for which reason Lao-tzu repeatedly uses water as a symbol of the Tao—which "loves and nourishes all things, but does not lord it over them," and which "flows always to that lowest level which men abhor." Read Theodore Schwenk's marvelous book *Sensitive Chaos* (London, Rudolph Steiner Press, 1965), which shows how the flow patterns of gases and liquids are basic to every form of life, how shells and bones are sculptures commemorating the forms of liquid lilt. This is the far-in meaning of Shakespeare's saying that "there is a tide in

the affairs of men which, taken at its flood, leads on to fortune."
For tune, for harmony, one follows the lead, the weight, of the
river.

> *Loco è laggiù da Belzebù remoto*
>   *tanto, quanto la tomba si distende,*
>   *che non per vista, ma per suono è noto*
> *D'un ruscelletto che quivi discende*
>   *per la buca d'un sasso, ch'egli ha roso*
>   *col corso ch'egli avvolge, e poco pende.*
> *Lo Duca ed io per quel cammino ascoso*
>   *entrammo a ritornar nel chiaro mondo.*

Inferno, 34. 127–34

Every project for self-transformation is a vicious circle. Dogen, a Zen master of the thirteenth century, said that spring does not become summer and, in the same way, firewood does not become ashes: there is spring, and then there is summer; there is firewood, and then there are ashes. By the same argument, a living being does not become a corpse, and an unenlightened person does not become a Buddha. Monday does not become Tuesday; one o'clock does not become four o'clock. Thus to try to become a Buddha, to attain enlightenment or liberation or supreme unselfishness, is like trying to wash off blood with blood, or polishing a brick to make a mirror. As Chuang-tzu said, "You see your egg and expect it to crow."

The selfishness of a selfish person is precisely that he is trying to become happier, stronger, wiser, braver, kindlier, and, in short, unselfish. "Is not your elimination of self," said Chuang-tzu, "a positive manifestation of self?" And again, "Those who say that they would have right without its correlate, wrong, or good government without its correlate, misrule, do not apprehend the great principles of the universe, nor the nature of all creation. One might as well talk of the existence of heaven without that of earth, or of the negative principle (*yin*) without the positive (*yang*), which is clearly impossible. Yet people keep on discussing it incessantly." The comment applies equally to all projects for self-improvement through gurus, meditations, yoga practice, self-acceptance, psychotherapy, and even total living-in-the-present. From such disciplines one can learn only that they are self-contradictory, like lifting both feet off the floor by pulling the ankles. And in this there is, perhaps, some value, for it releases our psychic and physical energy from impossible tasks for the possible: we can indeed plant seeds, gather fruit, build houses, sing songs, make love, and go on living until we stop.

Am I pointing this out to improve the state of mankind, and so contradicting myself? No, I am saying it so that we can be free to plant seeds and gather fruit. This has nothing to do with better or worse, progress or regress. These are judgments, and it is well said, "Judge not, that you be not judged; for with what judgment you judge, you shall be judged, and with what measure you measure, you shall be measured." And if you say, "But that is itself a judgment!" you are still judging. Is it *better* not to judge? No, it is simply living and dying, day and night, coming and going, a state of affairs in which there is neither the good by itself nor the bad by itself.

> The perfect Way is without difficulty,
> Save that it avoids picking and choosing.
> Only when you stop liking and disliking
> Will all be clearly understood. . . .
> Be not concerned with right and wrong.
> The conflict between right and wrong
> Is the sickness of the mind.

True, while we remain in the sickness of the mind, the "sickness" is "wrong," and the (wrong) conflict persists. But this is still judging the judgment, and judging the judgment of the judgment—the vicious circle and the infinite regression which Buddhists call *samsara*, the squirrel-cage situation of trying to have life without death and right without wrong. Such vicious circles cannot be stopped by preparations or methods or spiritual disciplines. These are all postponements. The only way to stop is to stop—instantly, now—by action, not thought. This stopping *can* happen, just as we *can* plant seeds and gather fruit—though no real action is something "done" by a conceptual "me." The division between doer and deed, knower and known, is a division of words, not of nature.

> Suffering alone exists, none who suffer;
> The deed there is, but no doer thereof;
> Nirvana is, but no one seeking it;
> The path there is, but none who travel it.

In short, the point is that every project for righting the world or oneself is a conceptual fantasy, because, while we remain in the world of concepts, we cannot identify right without the contrast of left or wrong. This is as true politically as it is psychologically, for the following of right-wing or left-wing ideologies diverts our attention from specific problems, just as projects for world improvement divert us from planting seeds and gathering fruit. In the name of such projects we obliterate whole populations for their own liberation, crowd criminals together in prisons for their rehabilitation, and isolate crazy people in asylums in the desperate hope that this will somehow make them sane.

Thus so-called black people have a thing against so-called

white people (I prefer the contrast of colored and discolored) because the Judaeo-Christian whites equate black with evil and crusade for a preposterous cosmos in which there will be right without left. Unhappily, the colored people have been infected with this religion, and are crusading (understandably enough) for something more than equal rights. But the more we become involved in possible debates between the rights and wrongs of these problems, the more we shall destroy each other for our own good, and neglect the planting of seeds and the gathering of fruit.

The "sickness of the mind" is the confusion of what can be said, or thought, with what can be done and with what actually happens. Release from this confusion comes with awareness, not thinking, but is frustrated by projects to be aware and not to think or, rather, to suspend thought. The idea that is it better, or "the goal," to be rid of this confusion is still confusion, and is called the stink of Zen. The concepts of health and sickness, good and evil, better and worse, have the same use and relation to life as those of long and short, high and low to carpentry: even a short piece of wood can be three inches long. Even cancer is called a growth, and when Ramana Maharshi was dying of cancer he resisted the doctors, saying, "It wants to grow, too. Let it." This is, perhaps, an extreme example of renunciation—not of love or energy—but of willing right as against wrong, and thus of renouncing one's own separateness from everything that happens, which is what Tillich called "the courage to be."

This attitude might be called a fatalism in which, however, there is no one fated: one's own subjective reactions are all of a piece with what, objectively, goes on—and therefore you do not intrude yourself upon the world. This is the Taoist attitude of *wu-wei*, of noninterference with the Tao, the Course of Nature. However, *wu-wei* is not a precept or a method to be followed or not followed: it is the realization that you yourself are not something apart from the Tao which can, or cannot, interfere with it. Experience your own decision as an event which happens like the opening of a bud.

Such a sudden flip of consciousness is rather like looking at nonobjective or abstract paintings as if they were colored photographs—it might be of markings in marble or of microscopic plants. Instantly, the whole quality of the painting changes: it becomes three-dimensional and vividly articulate. Even more remarkable is the change when subjective experience is taken as something happening of itself, like the wind, or—what comes to the same thing—when objective experience is taken as something which you are doing, like breathing.

ART WITH A CAPITAL A

Art, with a capital A, is a strictly modern and Western phenomenon. Not so long ago, say, about five hundred years, there were no museums, no galleries, no concert halls, and no special class of people to be known as Artists. What our museums now exhibit as the "art" of other cultures and ancient times are religious, magical, and household utensils exquisitely and lovingly made. These are by no means confined to objects of luxury made for the wealthy: they include the pottery, weaving, weapons, jewelry, and ritual tools of peasants. If there was any art in such times and cultures, it was simply the masterly production of things needed for everyday life. No one ever made anything for the express purpose of adorning a museum, of being shown in a gallery, or for being commended in newspapers. Scholars may manage to dig up a few exceptions to this observation, but the self-conscious practice of Art hardly existed before the advent of modern technology.

Today, many young painters, sculptors, and musicians are aware—sometimes clearly, sometimes obscurely—of the absurdity of "art for art's sake." We have, therefore, not only the theater of the absurd, but also the concert hall and gallery of the absurd. The formal scene of going to the concert came to a final crash when John Cage performed an entirely silent piano recital with the full ritual apparatus of evening dress, a Steinway, a score consisting wholly of rests, and an assistant to turn the pages. Be it said at the same time that John Cage is a musical genius, a man with divinely sensitive ears, who used this device in an attempt to persuade people to listen to the magical sounds that go on around us all the time. He was trying to clean our ears of melodic and harmonic prejudices.

Painters and sculptors are now catching up with him, though perhaps it all really began with Dada. With Pop Art and Minimal Art we have the gallery of the absurd, going beyond even the greatest excesses of abstract expressionism and action painting, with what (I hope) is the object of washing the eyes as Cage was cleaning ears. For Cage simply roars with laughter about his own projects (at himself, and not because he is hoaxing the public), and I wonder, sometimes, if Minimal Art sculptors are doing the same, or whether they conceive their productions to be "serious" in the same sense as a concert at which Bernstein is conducting Beethoven's Ninth Symphony is serious.

To clean out the prejudices of ears and eyes goes, indeed, beyond the domains of music, painting, sculpture, and drama to our basic orientation to life. Existence itself is a highly complex system of interwoven vibrations, and, from infancy, we have inherited the strongest prejudices as to which vibrations are permissible and acceptable and which are not. We are still at the point where pain and the prospect of death are as intolerable as was, say, Surrealism in 1930 or Cubism in 1910. It could therefore be argued that arts which infringe all traditional rules, and eventually get away with it, are preparing us for willing acceptance of the extinction of our species. Learning to enjoy their assaults upon our sensibilities will put us in a frame of mind to contemplate annihilation by H-bombs as a real gas.

But I am not being frivolous. It has always been known that the capacity to accept death in the midst of life—to swing with a conventionally intolerable vibration—is a source of immense creative power. "Unless a grain of corn falls into the ground and dies, it remains isolated. But if it dies, it brings forth much fruit." Or, as Goethe said it—

> *Und so lang du das nicht hast,*
> *Dieses: stirb und werde,*
> *Bist du nur ein trüber Gast*
> *Auf der dunklen Erde.*

"As long as you do not know how to die and come to life again, you are but a sorry traveler on this dark earth." And the Zen master Bunan:

> While living be a dead man, thoroughly dead.
> Then, whatever you do, just as you will, will be
>   right.

It is therefore my personal opinion that almost all avant-garde art forms of the twentieth century are transitional, in a peculiar and special sense. Obviously, all art is in transition, as is life itself. But the ear cleaning and eye washing that is now going on in the concert halls, galleries, and museums is in preparation for a return to the inseparability of art and every-day life. The paintings are vanishing into the walls: but they will be marvelous walls. In turn, the walls will vanish into the landscape: but the view will be ecstatic. And after that the viewer will vanish into the view.

However, an art inseparable from everyday life will not be

narrowly functional or utilitarian. By reason of electronics and automation we are moving—to the consternation of the Protestant conscience—into an age when there will hardly be any distinction between work and play. Mankind has to face the moral shock of realizing that masochistic work will be obsolete, for the slaves will no longer be people but machines, watched and tended by swinging and fascinated engineers. Art will therefore cease to be a propaganda calling attention to misery. It will use all the facilities of electronic technology to create an exuberant splendor which has not been seen since the days of Persian miniatures and arabesques, medieval stained glass, the illuminated manuscripts of the Celts, the enamels of Limoges, and the jewelry of Cellini.

The wheel extends the foot. Brush, chisel, hammer, and saw extend the hand. But electric circuitry extends the brain itself as an externalization of the nervous system, and will therefore perform wonders of art (that is, of playful patterns of energy) which have not heretofore been seen.

THE BUDDHISM OF ALDOUS HUXLEY

Aldous Huxley's last major work, the utopia *Island*, expressed his philosophy of life in its full maturity, and should be read as a philosophical essay rather than as a novel. During the years between the writing of *Ends and Means* and *Island*, I watched Huxley's development with intense interest. For at the beginning of his "mystical period" (about 1937) he was inclined to a type of spirituality which regards material existence as a fall into the gross bondage of the flesh, and differentiation and individuality as a sort of cosmic mistake—to be corrected by an ascetic yoga which restores the original state of homogenized, unitary consciousness. This is a spirituality, resembling Hinayana Buddhism and some types of Vedanta, which conceives the highest goal of life as a *nirvana* in which every form of multiplicity is wiped out.

But in *Island* Huxley came forth with a rich "spiritual materialism," which resembles nothing so much as the general outlook of Mahayana Buddhism—with which he was, of course, familiar. Mahayana (the "great course" or "vehicle"), which came to birth in India between about 100 BC and AD 400, is the form of Buddhism which migrated to China, Tibet, Mongolia, Korea, and Japan, and is contrasted by its followers with the

Hinayana (or "defective course"), which prevails in Southern Asia. The distinctive feature of Mahayana is that it regards *nirvana* as one and the same reality as the physical world (*samsara*), the difference between the two lying only in one's point of view or state of consciousness. It was this that enabled Mahayana Buddhism to be involved in and concerned with culture, and to be a way of life for lay men and women as well as monks.

Perhaps this is a merely subjective impression, but it has struck me (especially in Japan) that the attitude of Mahayana Buddhism, among all religions and philosophies, has been uniquely humane, openhearted, intellectually sophisticated and imaginative, and thoroughly civilizing—even without the benefits of Western technology. When I last visited Dr. Suzuki he spoke emphatically of the earthiness of Buddhism, and even went so far as to say that you could smell the essence of it in an incense prepared from aloes wood (*jinko*), which somehow distills and concentrates all one's happy memories of the smell of wood and trees.

Thus in Mahayana Buddhism the highest form of man is not the ascetic *arhan*, who remains in almost perpetual contemplation, but the bodhisattva, for whom everyday life and activity are entirely consistent with being in the state of *nirvana*, and who lives in this world out of compassion for others, working to share with them his own state of vision. It is somehow significant that this philosophy appealed to such a highly cultured Westerner as Huxley, with his deep concern, not only for the arts and literature, but also for the sociological, educational, and economic problems of the modern world.

I do not say this to claim Huxley as a convert to a form of Buddhism, since Mahayanists have seldom any interest in sectarian propaganda and totting up adherents, their disciplines being closer to such inquiries as psychology and philosophy than to militant religions. For Mahayana is not so much an ideology as a complex of methods for correcting our perception and conception of life. Its essence is not a theory but a realization—almost a sensation—of relativity, that is, of the mutual interdependence of all things and events.

Human consciousness is normally fixed or "hung up" (a perfect Americanism for the Buddhist sense of "attachment") on the apparent separateness of things, including oneself. It is a type of attention to the world which screens out, or ignores, the fact that all phenomena *go with* each other inseparably—in the same way as back and front or the poles of a magnet. Thus we do not normally realize that being and nonbeing, life and death, self and other, solid and space, pulse and interval, go with each other in the same basic unity. We are therefore tormented with the anxiety that death may overcome life, that nonbeing may swallow being, or that the viewpoint which we call "self" may vanish, and leave only a world of objects or "others."

This view of the world as a mere assemblage of separate things and a sequence of distinct events gives the individual the feeling that he is no more than a temporary *part* of reality—a thing among things. According to Mahayana there are no things, considered as separate entities. So-called things are gestures of the universe, that is, of an energy system which is the only real "self" that we have, but which we cannot define or classify—in the same way that we cannot (and need not) look directly into our own eyes. Yet it is possible to be aware that this indefinable energy system, which, in its entirety, is what and who each individual truly is.

Such an awareness opens up for us the possibility of participation in all the games of life—the patterns and gestures of the universe—without anxiety and with compassion, realizing that every other self is, under the surface, the same self as our own. And such compassion, as "feeling/suffering-with," is not mere pity in the sense that "misery loves company." It is grounded in the knowledge that existence is basically exuberance—that "energy is eternal delight," and that, improbable as it may seem, every form of being lies somewhere on the vast spectrum of ecstasy which, in Mahayana, is called the *sambhogakaya*, "The Body of Total Bliss."

Many people believe that without anxiety there would be no motivation for a creative life. "If I am to be good, someone must beat me." But creation is not mere flight from punishment and fear, and no one wants the surgeon to be anxious, with his knife in a trembling hand. The problem is that we are now wielding the incredible surgical instrument of technology with trembling hands, and what concerned Huxley was that such power cannot be handled constructively by anxious and alienated men with a fundamentally hostile attitude to nature. Mahayana Buddhists never had our technology; but they had art, and practiced it to high perfection (in China and Japan) as a cooperation between man and nature—indeed, as a work of nature itself. What if the same realization—that science can be the work of nature, and that the individual is one body with his environment—could become the informing spirit of Western technology?

D. T. SUZUKI: THE "MIND-LESS" SCHOLAR

I have never had a formal teacher (*guru* or *roshi*) in the spiritual life—only an exemplar, whose example I have not really followed because no sensitive person likes to be mimicked. That exemplar was Suzuki Daisetsu, at once the subtlest and the simplest person I have known. His intellectual and spiritual mood or atmosphere I found wholly congenial, although I never knew him really intimately and although I myself am an entirely different kind of person. Suzuki introduced me to Zen when I first read his *Essays in Zen Buddhism* in mid-adolescence, and in the years that followed I read everything he wrote with fascination and delight. For what he said was always unexpected and open-ended. He did not travel in the well-worn ruts of philosophical and religious thought. He rambled, he digressed, he dropped hints, he left you suspended in mid-air, he astonished you with his learning (which was prodigious) and yet charmed you with scholarship handled so lightly and unpretentiously. For I found in the engagingly disorganized maze of his writings the passage to a Garden of Reconciled Opposites.

He showed why Zen is immensely difficult and perfectly easy, why it is at once impenetrable and obvious, why the infinite and eternal is exactly the same as your own nose at this moment, why morals are both essential and irrelevant to the spiritual life, and why *jiriki* (the way of personal effort) comes finally to the same point as *tariki* (the way of liberation through pure faith). The trick in following Suzuki was never to "stay put," as if you had at last got his point and were on firm ground—for the next moment he would show you that you had missed it altogether.

Suzuki was also outside the ordinary ruts in that, without any show of eccentricity, he did not present himself in the stereotype of the usual "Zen personality" which one finds among Japanese monks. Anyone visiting him for the first time, expecting to find an old gentleman with flashing eyes, sitting in a bare *shibui*-type room, and ready to engage you in swift and vigorous repartee, would have been very much surprised. For Suzuki, with his miraculous eyebrows, was more like a Chinese Taoist scholar—a sort of bookish Lao-tzu—gifted, as all good Taoists are, with what can only be called metaphysical humor. Every so often his eyes twinkled as if he had seen the Ultimate Joke, and as if, out of compassion for those who had not, he were refraining from laughing out loud.

He lived in the Western-style section of his home in Kamakura completely surrounded with piles of books and papers. This scholarly disarray was spread through several rooms, in each of which he was writing a separate book, or separate chapters of one book. He could thus move from room to room without having to clear away all his reference materials when feeling inclined to work upon one project rather than another; but somehow his admirable secretary Miss Okamura (who was actually an *apsara* sent down from the Western Paradise to take care of him in his old age) seemed to know where everything was.

Suzuki spoke slowly, deliberately, and gently in excellent

English with a slight and to our ears, very pleasing Japanese accent. In conversation, he almost always explained himself with the aid of pen and paper, drawing diagrams to illustrate his points and Chinese characters to identify his terms. Though a man of wonderful patience, he had a genius for deflating windy argument or academic pedantry without giving offense. I remember a lecture where a member of the audience asked him, "Dr. Suzuki, when you use the word 'reality,' are you referring to the relative reality of the physical world, or to the absolute reality of the transcendental world?" He closed his eyes and went into that characteristic attitude which some of his students call "doing a Suzuki," for no one could tell whether he was in deep meditation or fast asleep. After about a minute's silence, though it seemed longer, he opened his eyes and said, "Yes."

During a class on the basic principles of Buddhism: "This morning we come to Fourth Noble Truth...called Noble Eightfold Path. First step of Noble Eightfold Path is called *sho ken. Sho ken* means Right View. All Buddhism is really summed up in Right View, because Right View is having no special view, no fixed view. Second step of Noble Eightfold Path..." (and here there was a long pause) "Oh, I forget second step. You look it up in the book." In the same vein, I remember his address to the final meeting of the 1963 World Congress of Faiths at the old Queen's Hall in London. The theme was "The Supreme Spiritual Ideal," and after several speakers had delivered themselves of volumes of hot air, Suzuki's turn came to take the platform. "When I was first asked," he said, "to talk about the Supreme Spiritual Ideal I did not exactly know what to answer. Firstly, I am just a simple-minded countryman from a faraway corner of the world suddenly thrust into the midst of this hustling city of London, and I am bewildered and my mind refuses to work in the same way that it does when I am in my own land. Secondly, how can a humble person like myself talk about such a grand thing as the Supreme Spiritual Ideal? . . . Really I do not know what Spiritual is, what Ideal is, and what Supreme Spiritual Ideal is." Whereupon he devoted the rest of his speech to a description of his house and garden in Japan, contrasting it with the life of a great city. This from the translator of the *Lankavatara Sutra*! And the audience gave him a standing ovation.

Being well aware of the relativity and inadequacy of all opinions, he would never argue. When a student tried to provoke him into a discussion of certain points upon which the celebrated Buddhist scholar Junjiro Takakusu differed from him, his only comment was, "This is very big world; plenty of room in it for both Professor Takakusu and myself." Well, perhaps there was one argument—when the Chinese scholar Hu Shih accused him of obscurantism (in asserting that Zen could not be expressed in rational language) and of lacking a sense of history. But in the course of a very courteous reply Suzuki said, "The Zen master, generally speaking, despises those who indulge in word- or idea-mongering, and in this respect Hu Shih and myself are great sinners, murderers of Buddhas and patriarchs; we are both destined for hell."

I have never known a great scholar and intellectual so devoid of conceit. When I first met Suzuki, I was flabbergasted that he asked me (aged twenty) how to prepare a certain article, and that when I was brash enough to give my advice he followed it. Academic pomposity and testiness were simply not in him. Thus certain American sinologists, who make a fine art of demolishing one another with acrimonious footnotes, are apt to go into a huff about his rather casual use of documentation and "critical apparatus," and to speak of him as a mere "popular-izer." They do not realize that he genuinely loved scholarship and thus made no show of "being a scholar." He had no interest in using bibliography as a gimmick for boosting his personality.

Perhaps the real spirit of Suzuki could never be caught from his writings alone: one had to know the man. Many readers complain that his work is so un-Zen-like—verbose, discursive, obscure, and cluttered with technicalities. A Zen monk once explained to me that the attitude of *mushin* (the Zen style of unself-consciousness) was like the Japanese carpenter who can build a house without a blueprint. I asked, "What about the man who draws a blueprint without making a plan for it?" This was, I believe, Suzuki's attitude in scholarship: he thought, he intellectualized, he pored over manuscripts and dictionaries as any Zen monk might sweep floors in the spirit of *mushin*. In his own words, "Man is a thinking reed but his great works are done when he is not calculating and thinking. 'Childlikeness' has to be restored with long years of training in the art of self-forgetfulness. When this is attained, man thinks yet he does not think. He thinks like showers coming down from the sky; he thinks like the waves rolling on the ocean; he thinks like the stars illuminating the nightly heavens; he thinks like the green foliage shooting forth in the relaxing spring breeze. Indeed, he is the showers, the ocean, the stars, the foliage."

ABOUT THE AUTHOR

Alan Watts, who held both a master's degree in theology and a doctorate of divinity, is best known as an interpreter of Zen Buddhism in particular, and of Indian and Chinese philosophy in general. Standing apart, however, from sectarian membership, he has earned the reputation of being one of the most original and "unrutted" philosophers of the century. He was the author of some twenty books on the philosophy and psychology of religion, including *The Way of Zen*; *The Wisdom of Insecurity*; *Nature, Man and Woman*; *The Book*; *Beyond Theology*; *In My Own Way*; and *Cloud Hidden, Whereabouts Unknown*. He died in 1973.